TO JohnOLSON,

A GREAT FRIEND,
WHOSE INFINITE
CURIOSITY ABOUT LIFE
IS CONTINUOUSLY
INSPIRING.....

Wandering the Garden of Technology and Passion
John Marx, Architect

Wandering the Garden of Technology and Passion
John Marx, Architect

Introduction by Chris I. Yessios
Written by Pierluigi Serraino

Balcony Press, Los Angeles

First Edition

Published in the United States of America in 2011 by Balcony Press.

For information address
Balcony Media, Inc.
512 E. Wilson Avenue, Suite 213
Glendale, California 91206
www.balconypress.com

Designed by Sarah Beach
Printing and production by Navigator Cross-media
Printed in South Korea

Wandering the Garden of Technology and Passion
© 2011 Pierluigi Serraino / John Marx

Library of Congress Control Number
ISBN 978-1-890449-56-8

TABLE OF CONTENTS

Premise: An Architectural Practice in Five Slices

The literature of architecture is a genre codified in few well-established forms. Monographs, historical and contemporary surveys, theory manifestos, and coffee table publications are the building blocks of a body of printed reflections and illustrations that architects rely on to stake their own identity as cultural producers within broad human endeavors. Rather than assessing those forms as obsolete, the belief here is that alternative ways to account for architecture exist. This book is a first step in the expansion of those literary boundaries. Its subject matter is contemporary architectural practice observed through one case study: the design architect John Marx, founding design principal of Form4, a firm rooted in San Francisco, California.

While architecture is as ancient as humankind, its practice has undergone epochal changes over time. Urban geographer David Harvey aptly described this compression of time and space in his landmark title *The Condition of Postmodernity*, describing how architecture has been catapulted to a terrain unforeseeable just a generation ago. Architects are caught between the economic imperatives of private capital and their own idealism for a better environment, something they have internalized since their college years. If it can be said that dealing with financial resources has been a structural condition of architecture since the Industrial Revolution, the digital shift has only made that schism more pungent. The two poles around which architects organize their careers come down to architecture as profession versus architecture as art. However, there is something unique about architecture that singles it out from the other fine arts. It does not qualify as a hobby done in spare time; instead a commission is needed for its apparatus to start up. Without that trigger architecture cannot chart its course.

Five chapters divide the work of John Marx that outline the wide-ranging and biographical conditions of being an architect today. These episodes are structured around themes that cross-section his output, highlighting issues of general interest and avoiding the classic chronological trope so ubiquitous in tales of an architect's accomplishments. Marx's design impulse is the undercurrent throughout these sections. It is through design that architects have the greatest chance to bring relevance to their work and affect people's lives in significantly positive ways.

John Marx and the Digital Revolution

By Chris I. Yessios

In the early '90s, a couple of years after form•Z was born on February 14, 1991, as we were looking for testimonials of what people were doing with our software, we came across some particularly impressive architectural models and images produced by a young designer called John Marx. At the time John was working for Hoover Associates in San Francisco. I still remember the images of the Steamfitters Union building, which almost looked like it was rendered by hand using watercolor. I later learned that John was particularly skilled in watercolor before he picked up his computer skills and he seems to have carried this bias in his early computer renderings, a style he achieved with Photoshop, an application that he also learned well concurrently with form•Z. Observing his early images together with the ones he has been producing more recently, one can immediately sense the evolution of an impressive mastery of the digital tools.

Those of us that have more or less dedicated our professional lives to the development of digital tools are delighted when we come across gifted designers like John Marx. While a significant number of headline architects have recognized the potential and have embraced digital tools ever since their early days, most of them have done so by relying on their assistants to drive the electronic machines for them. A few, and John Marx is one of the most notable among them, became proficient users themselves. The most accomplished did not simply allow the machines to drive their imagination, but instead, they stretched the capabilities of the digital tools into areas never consciously intended by their developers. John Marx is one of the most distinguished and successful digital designers who, by his own recognition, couldn't have been the designer he has become if he hadn't embraced and mastered digital technologies to the extent he has.

It is not the scope of this write up to critique John's work, which is done elsewhere in this book. However, I can't help commenting on some apparent qualities that make the "invasion" of the digital tools, as some like to call it, well worth it. In the earlier days, we used to ask the question: "Have the digital tools helped us produce better architecture, yet?" Looking at John's designs the answer is an undeniable "yes." John has definitely grown into the excellent designer he is to a large extent thanks to his mastery of the digital tools. At the same time he helped improve the usability of these tools. He did so, not by actually getting involved with programming, but as an insightful user, by uncovering and demonstrating creative ways with which imaginative forms and spaces, significantly beyond what was achievable before, could be synthesized with ease. He has come a long way since his initial watercolor-looking designs. Some of his most recent projects almost look like music that is not yet frozen, to borrow from Goethe.

In the early days of computer-aided design research, Nick Negreponte's book "The Architecture Machine" had become our bible and had influenced our thinking. He wrote about computer tools so artificially intelligent that they could form partnerships with human designers. While many of Negreponte's promises (or maybe prophecies) remain utopias, we have to credit him with having initiated the debate about the desired relationships between human designers and the machines.

Since the early days of CAD development, regardless of whether "D" was taken to mean "drafting" or "design," we debated whether digital tools should be in the image of man, that is imitating established professional practices, or whether they should be introducing new, more effective methods, which would require retraining the professionals. While the debate has remained inconclusive to-date, most of us have come to recognize that the ideal solutions would come from a combination of the two. While we want to take complete advantage of all those capabilities offered by the computer, even when they may deviate from established practices, we want to do it in ways that can be intuitively embraced by humans, without extensive retraining.

In all this we have to recognize that personalities can vary drastically. This has led to the axiom that there can never be a digital system capable of making everybody equally happy. Different individuals will be attracted to different digital systems. This holds true at least for the currently established professionals. They are the ones that learned their trade before the digital tools became commonplace. But what about the next generation of designers who are being trained with more or less mature digital tools? Will there be more uniformity regarding the digital tools they will be comfortable with? This discussion goes beyond the scope of this article and if we take into consideration that the different digital tools also tend to become more and more similar every day, by accepting de facto standards that have evolved in professional practices, then maybe the issue is less significant than what it first appears.

Within this spectrum of present and future design personalities, it appears that John Marx is an exception, whom we, developers of design tools, would like to see become the rule. As a novice designer trained during the post-modern era with a heavy dose of anthropology and environmental psychology, his graphic tools included watercolor, in addition to pencil. He was already a pretty mature designer when he encountered computers in the early '90s and he took the time to train himself mainly in two programs: form•Z and Photoshop. I need a better word than "train" to express how John involved himself with form•Z's 3D modeling. He dug into the behavior of the different operations and sought to uncover their logic and above all their potential. He was frequently delighted when he was discovering possibilities that had been challenging to the manual means he had experienced thus far. He made contact with us soon there after with comments, questions, and suggestions, which I still remember as being impressively insightful and led us to major improvements in a number of our tools. As already mentioned, soon we had the pleasure of observing some of John's designs, which demonstrated an impressive grasp of the tools and creative usage that went significantly beyond our original intentions.

Soon enough John Marx also got involved with teaching at the Berkeley Department of Architecture. Those were the days when Instructors were actually teaching students how to use and how to be creative with digital tools, and John was definitely one of the best. Having dug deeply into the potential of digital tools for his own work, he also developed an admirable ability to transmit these skills and enthusiasm to his students. These ex-students are the new generation of designers that subsequently took jobs with established professionals and helped them apply digital tools in their practice.

Today, the use of digital tools is widespread and nobody argues against them or expresses the old fears that they will de-humanize architecture and that they will lead to franchise architecture (similar computer-generated designs repeated all over the world). The only concern we hear today is that architecture may have gone too far in producing forms that are difficult for the man on the street to comprehend, as they are produced with mathematical formulas that only advanced mathematicians and engineers understand. This raises the question of who are (or ought to be) the decisive participants not only when digital tools are used but also, and more importantly, when these tools are designed and developed. From the point of view of this text, the question becomes how can we continue involving the John Marxes of the profession as we develop the next generation of tools.

Before we can start addressing this question it helps to first identify the trends that have manifested themselves in recent years. There seem to be two directions, which are ideally complementary, but in practice compete with each other. On the one hand, are the tools that enhance our ability to invent new forms. They are labeled parametric, generative, genetic, etc. and they capitalize on mathematics to produce shapes that traditional manual means cannot conceive. We tend to call them design-oriented systems. On the other hand, are the building information modeling (or BIM) systems. These typically have little concern about the generation of innovative forms but rather concentrate on recording and making readily available the data required to support the production of construction drawings, engineering calculations, and ultimately the management of the completed building.

Which approach is correct? There are serious advocates on both sides, but a detailed discussion would again be beyond the scope of this text. Let me just say that, ideally, we should combine the two. Easily said but hard to do. Actually, it would be rather paradoxical to combine the two, given their contradictory philosophies. The design approach encourages innovation and thrives when original forms are invented. The BIM approach requires pre-existing knowledge and more or less standardized details. To automate the marriage of these two will require artificial intelligence breakthroughs no less utopian than the propositions of the Architecture Machine. In the meantime, human intelligence as it is applied to the daily practice of the design professions will do and once again John Marx is offering us a paradigm of how it can be done.

It is widely recognized that BIM is an attitude and a way of organizing and operating an architectural practice, rather than a digital system that automatically applies BIM technology. Actually, all of the commercial systems that claim BIM capabilities were marketed as BIM only after the term became fashionable. In practice, BIM systems have been implemented successfully only where the organization of an office subscribes to BIM principles. Conversely, whenever a design team adheres to BIM principles, the positive results of BIM can be achieved even with applications that are not labeled BIM, but offer modeling robustness and high accuracy. It is reported that John Marx fits the latter paradigm.

John Marx's practice does not use BIM applications but rather conventional drafting programs for producing construction drawings. The data comes directly from the 3D models and becomes the basis not only for the construction details but also for the structural calculations and the environmental analyses. Anybody who has observed the complexity of many of John's designs must ultimately be impressed by the efficiency of the organization at the Form4 firm. It is questionable whether current commercial BIM systems would have been capable of handling the complexity of John's designs. We need BIM systems that can extrapolate even complex designs and extract the data that is required for further studies of a structure. To do this, a dialogue between developers and creative professionals is necessary.

The dreams we had 30-40 years ago were not exactly in the direction the digital tools have taken today. They were placing more emphasis on production, while much of what we have today enhances our creativity and helps us produce more exciting architecture. This makes one wonder what the future holds. Without question we continue to dream of machines that will automatically execute all those tedious tasks that are no fun to do. However, if the trends continue, the chances are that there will also be digital tools that are, above all, inventors of forms that no human has imagined before. The one thing certain is that, whatever the future holds, it will only result from an intimate collaboration between sensitive developers and designers of the caliber of John Marx.

1

Origins

Place-making, an emotional experience of architecture, is what design architect John Marx has been pursuing ever since he left his native Illinois to settle in San Francisco. The clarity of his approach to space is the result of years of filtering the early educational messages about community identity, the cachet of design stardom, and the mythologies of computer technology, blending what remained with his distinct individual sensibility. At the other end of this personal itinerary is the national and international body of work open to public appreciation and critical scrutiny. Marx belongs to that generation of architects who witnessed the morphing of their pencil into a mouse, their drafting table into a desktop. The survivors of this epochal transition still standing are few and far between. Yet most unique about his journey is his remarkable aesthetic consistency and the organic of his architecture over the years, in the translation of the painterly visions of the early days of his career into the full-blown propositions produced today.

His buildings are as eclectic as the sources that inspire them, yet a common ambition is present in all of them: to design a "place you want to be in." Whether a suspended garden on a high-rise in Sao Paulo, Brazil, the courtyard of an office space in Pune, India, or a swimming pool at a health club in San Diego, California, John Marx always strives to generate an emotional connection for the users. Such determination is partly rooted in his reaction to the bleak austerity of early seventies modernism that was ravaging the western world as he was growing up in the Midwest, and partly in the profound belief that architecture is central for the improvement of the human experience, both programmatically and as a fine and ethereal art form, rather than a simply utilitarian background for multifarious activities. Despite the fact that the fanfare of the architecture press is built upon those prized commissions rarely available even to the very restricted circle of "star-architects," Marx's inventions are centered around being of benefit to the public at large with accessible yet poetic design. His commissions fall between service firms and elite design studios. His practice, by his own definition, is a reflective practice.

Flow, asymmetry, and layering are the three main themes in Marx's architecture. The basis for this comes from many sources in the history of architecture. The formal magnitude of Frank Lloyd Wright's Robie House in Chicago of 1911 and the un-built brick house by Mies van der Rohe of 1923 are two modernist landmarks showcasing the carefully orchestrated dynamic fluidity that Marx is so intensely concerned with. Both projects rely on the unlocking of the traditional static grid to enclose space and unleash the aesthetic energy embedded in a formal system that has scripted architectural expressions for centuries. This also explains the appeal of Constructivism to Marx's imaginary world. He is inspired by the Russian movement's idea of bringing order to what at first glance appears to be the chaotic assemblage of design elements.

one

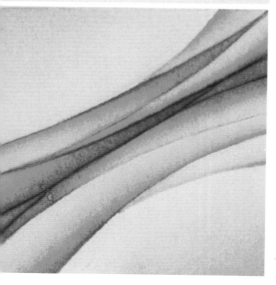

The Art Nouveau movement and the Austrian Secession—including architects such as Otto Wagner, Jose Maria Olbrich-are historical precedents from the turn-of-the-century modernist movement that fascinates Marx. The study of nature and its patterns of energy is the origin of a repertoire of forms endowed with flow and vigor, which in turn have shaped his buildings. The fluidity of that geometry and its transitional quality from the large scale to the smallest level of detail brought about innovative results of great resonance to Marx: this fluidity is found everywhere in his own designs. Concurrently, the oeuvre of Japanese architect Shin Takamastu was an important early influence, less because of dynamic power, but-metaphorically speaking-more about the crafting of the building as a jewel box, the scale of the detail and the way it interlocks and interrelates with its adjacency. Marx also admires the work of Swiss architect Mario Botta for its graphic strength, the Italian master Carlo Scarpa for its dense originality, the New Yorker Richard Meier for the way he pulls buildings apart, their size, and lack of ornamentation, and lastly, the entire portfolio of the Spanish engineer and architect Santiago Calatrava for the gracefulness of his curvilinear world. This last reference uncovers a recognizable element of his style: curves occupy a special place in Marx's work. For him, they follow the flow, they speak to people; a curve alone can be the highlight in the whole building, poetic in an emotional, intuitive sense. Although often costly, curved architectural elements hold inherent seductive beauty and extraordinary efficiency, to the point of becoming a hallmark in his spatiality. By his account, a straight wall lacks these traits, whereas a curved one generates dynamist spaces. These diagrammatic curves are initially conceived in three dimensions, while they still lack any material definition. Furthermore, curves fuse discrete spaces that host programmatic requirements and follow the flow of people and what they do.

In his formative years, watercolors and photography were Marx's vehicles for exploring his distinct imagery, and the refinement of this painterly awareness would later shape his architectural world. Marx's love affair with watercolors started in high school, where he initially focused on the representation of external reality, or the physical world as is. These visual exercises were discoveries of scale and detail that would soon mature into a specific attitude toward the design of building envelopes. While in college, Marx began experimenting with the abstract, partly because of his exposure to art history and non-representational modern paintings, and partly due to a quest for self-expression. These watercolors were more than thumbnails representing made-up building parts arranged in visually engaging patterns. Even the natural landscapes were designed. They were based on a collection of experiences rather than an actual place or object. Marx remarks: "The more you see, the more you are challenged by interesting things that compel you. It is a very intuitive attraction."

This intense view is the undercurrent feeding his work to this day. What generated those abstractions was the marriage of watercolors and photography. His fascination with the abstract relationships between different pieces and parts of things in the form of composition took on a life of its own and forged the mold through which all of his architecture would be cast. This kaleidoscope of bits and pieces is the template for the spaces to come and the texture of their enclosures, and provides the common themes that find their way into the building. In addition to photography, there are two other devices behind the compositional dynamics of Marx's works: cropping, and the critical interaction between what is represented and the frame itself. This dynamic is what gets translated into architecture and turned into inhabited forms.

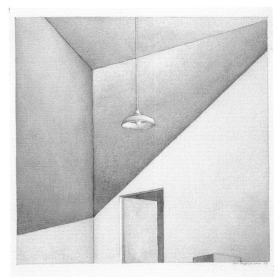

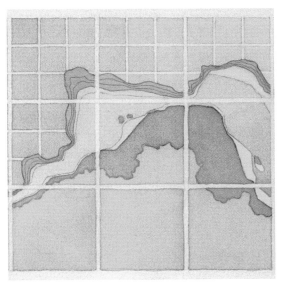

Folded into the larger meta-category of sustainability is that other invariable behind all Marx projects: daylight. It is his firm belief that: "For any building to be successful you should not have to turn the light on during the day."

Daylight has to celebrate the seduction of those activated volumes. For Marx, the quality of the architecture, just like the quality of photography or the quality of any digital renderings, depends wholly on the way light gets into the building, and how the building picks up that light. This awareness was further enhanced when he transitioned to computer-aided-design in 1991 and became proficient in 3D modeling. He began to understand that setting up the lighting is the divider between a powerful rendering and an underwhelming depiction, regardless of the merit of the design. Failure to orchestrate lighting in an evocative fashion results in a lifeless representation of the architectural idea and a client unresponsive to the design vision.

Between his early association with the corporate environment through design firms Kaplan, McLaughlin and Diaz (KMD) and Hellmuth, Obata + Kassabaum (HOK), and his exposure to the regionalist practice of renowned architect Warren Callister, Marx learned the trade and challenges associated with mid-to large-scale offices. Brief stints at local Bay Area offices Hoover Design and DES were the prelude for the fine-tuning of the digital design process that now propels the portfolio of Form4 Inc., the firm Marx founded with three other partners in 1999. In the phase before Form4, a progression of projects trailed the transition between his first tentative steps as a design personality and the professional confidence of the middle years, where sizeable international commissions were routine endeavor for the up-and-coming designer.

Marx's first solo design job out of school was in the early 1980s at Wm B Coney Architects. He designed the un-built Macomb City fire station, showcasing a grand barrel-vaulted roof highlighted through a beaux-art watercolor. A Mondrian-esque pattern gave character to its ends. With the Bishop Ranch Museum of 1989, his starting point was an axonometric view to fight the flatness of the elevation. While still in analog mode, Marx displayed complete command of the rendering techniques that would reach full maturity in his later work on the computer. In this early project, Marx's architecture starts to disengage the Post-modern stricture of representation with the introduction of subdued luminosity, precursor to the in-depth lighting explorations of the ensuing years. The Steamfitters Union Hall of 1991, although designed using the pencil-on-Mylar technique under Takamatsu's influence, began this transition from analog to digital. He attempted alternative rendering ideas while working for Hoover Associates, designing building piping systems under pressure, from simple systems all the way to mega-projects such as oil refineries. Tilt-up concrete technology and a series of tubes originally in stainless steel (with the top tube as a shading device) generated the dominant image. The underlying theme was the idea of the building as a machine. It is with this project that the first instance of his pioneering approach to combine the 3D-modeling program form•Z with the image-editing Photoshop took place. Marx taught himself both applications and originated a string of novel renderings that singled him out from his peers. Furthermore, this unique skill-set, realized through architectural practice, opened opportunities for Marx to teach courses in digital design at the College of Environmental Design at the University of California Berkeley, from 1995 until 2001.

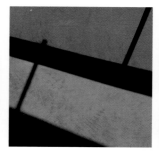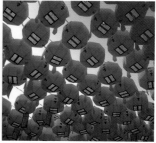

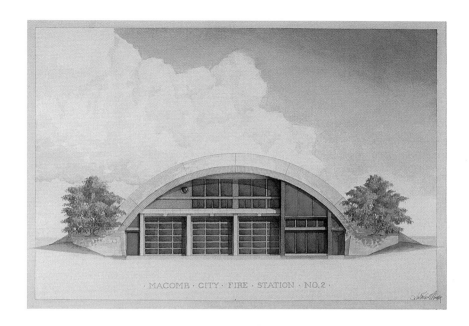

MACOMB · CITY · FIRE · STATION · NO.2 ·

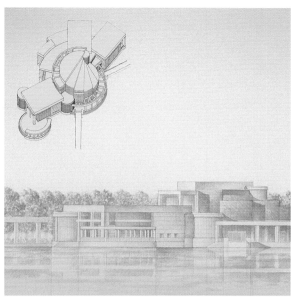

In 1996, Marx served as project designer for a two-week competition at KMD for the design of the GLOBO headquarters, a large media conglomerate in Brazil. It was the precursor to a massing strategy that would soon reappear in numerous other projects. Marx honed a powerful digital design technique during this competition that yielded striking images at the infancy of computer visualization. The un-built winning entry featured a landmark situated on a parcel of land facing a main river and a major freeway from where the building would be a billboard at night. Over twenty massing iterations preceded the final scheme, which included a titanium sphere housing a conference center and crowning a 100-foot-tall atrium. Movies from the GLOBO Company were to be projected on the sphere in order to create iconic buzz. The solar orientation of the tower was such that its knife-edge (smaller area facing the sun) pointed west and the angle of incidence of the sun on the glass was at its maximum. The un-built competition for the Korean Industrial Design Center (KIDC) designed during the KMD competition was about a program-intensive tower in a vast compound. The site called for an L-shaped building, undulating and curving with towers, the forms playing off of the trees along the river. A conical shape at the bottom of the first floor went up three stories, a metaphorical attempt to mimic the rocks and the river, with three different areas targeted as "the place you want to be," following Marx's intent.

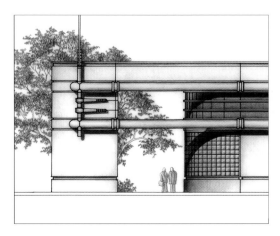

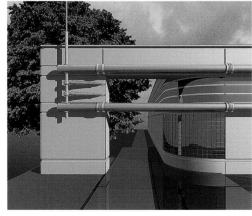

Between the extreme practice models of the solo office of Australian architect Glenn Murcutt, and the large scale conglomerates such as Skidmore, Owings & Merrill sits the mid-size organization, like Form4. Marx is a principal of the firm, together with two other architects. A fourth principal left shortly after the founding of the firm. The unlikely trio navigates market turbulences and differences of opinions by way of a quasi-religiously observed calendar of every-other-day lunches, where the sharp edges of working together are filed off in a spirit of camaraderie. An intuitive non-verbal balance of personalities, instead of a formal mission statement, informs the priorities and directions of their workplace. Through an amicable and fluid division of labor the workflow is parceled out in such a way that each principal exerts considerable control in his realm of expertise. Routinely performing conceptual design through working drawings, Form4 is a generalist firm. They believe that the universality of good design remains an independent project: all building types have the potential to be the much-sought-after "place to be."

Marx has only continued to excel since purchasing his first computer in 1991 with the form•Z 1.04 release, a general-purpose modeler of great acclaim among signature architects, yet still with only rudimentary rendering capabilities. This rite of passage between the drawing board and the desktop generated profound changes in his architectural explorations, in the increased accuracy of translation between the conceptual phase and the execution of ideas in working drawings, and in tangible material rewards. This leap into the digital mode made possible the formation of an enlightened professional model where sound business practices and deep-seated design aspirations mutually reinforce one another.

The high level of principal participation in the design process is what all the founders agree upon, in spite of differences in their individual characters. While a senior principal may attend almost all construction meetings, a younger princple may follow projects from the early stages to final occupancy. Conversely, Marx, in his role as senior designer, does the bulk of the 3D modeling, yet removes himself from construction meetings. In this practice model, Marx maintains control over the design, which he does on the computer using the latest release of form•Z Renderzone Plus. The Design Development and Construction Documents drawings are based on the computer model. This streamlined process yields sizeable financial rewards, in addition to preserving the integrity of the design idea from conception to execution. The geometry of the building is fully described in the digital model: the offset of the trim and the dimensions and spacing of the mullions, for example, appear in the computer model. The production team is free from approximations of interpreting a concept design into quantifiable form. The measurements are already there and the translation of the model in working drawings is remarkably accurate. In the days of analog design, Marx spent half of his time as project designer insuring proper translation of the design into working drawings. Once he became proficient in digital modeling, his time investment dropped significantly. This efficiency of design translation is paramount to making a convincing business case for the adoption of such a process. By Marx's own admission, the problem with the older system is that you lose such efficiency once it is handed off to a crew who must then interpret the model it has received before in turn handing it off to another crew. Marx's efficient system is based on the fact that the same person who builds the computer model completes the original design.

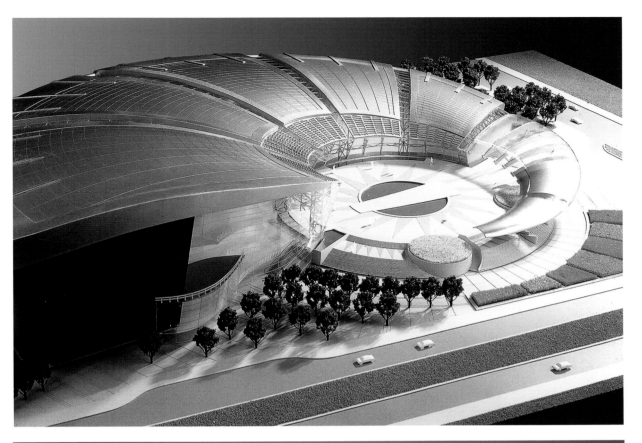

Even before taking the leap to becoming professionally independent, Marx tried out his place-making strategy with the design of the Guangzhou Opera in China in his last year as lead designer at Kaplan McLaughlin Diaz in 1999. Although the project won the competition, it was never realized due to unfortunate political circumstances—U.S. missiles had mistakenly hit the Chinese Embassy in Belgrade. The digital process was in its infancy at the time, and a simple form•Z model was produced with sketches drawn on printouts. Facing a large river, the performance facility sits on a podium, where the plaza is raised. All the lobbies are inside of the glass edge and face the open area. The centrifugal force springing from the center of the circular plaza shapes the plan and the three dimensional development of the sculptural roof.

This is hardly a trivial detail in a time where discourse on the transformative potential of implementing strategies for Building Information Modeling (BIM) is in full swing. Author, Dana K. Smith writes: "No commercially available software application or technology platform is capable of containing all of the information created about a building throughout its useful life and making it accessible to appropriate stakeholders in real time demand. More significantly, none is in development. The unmistakable trend in building information modeling software development is toward distributed building information models created by highly specialized software tools that are designed to work together."

With a far more modest financial investment than the grafting of an entirely new technology on a work flow, and more exclusive control of the conceptual model, Marx's methods might be the closest the practice of architecture can get to an idea of integrated design, since all projects coming out of the Form4 office are produced in the vein of models that capture the design intent of the designer and is also produced by the designer.

Practicing architecture is a form of mediated autobiography. The first impressions of the world, the initial realizations about the self, and the discoveries of childhood and adolescence frame the sensibility of the designer. The creative potential of those early experiences in forging a mindset for a reality to be imagined take the work of a lifetime to be realized. And to paraphrase T.S. Eliot in *Little Gidding*, during their lifelong journey, architects will endlessly explore in order to eventually arrive back where they started, and then know themselves for the first time.

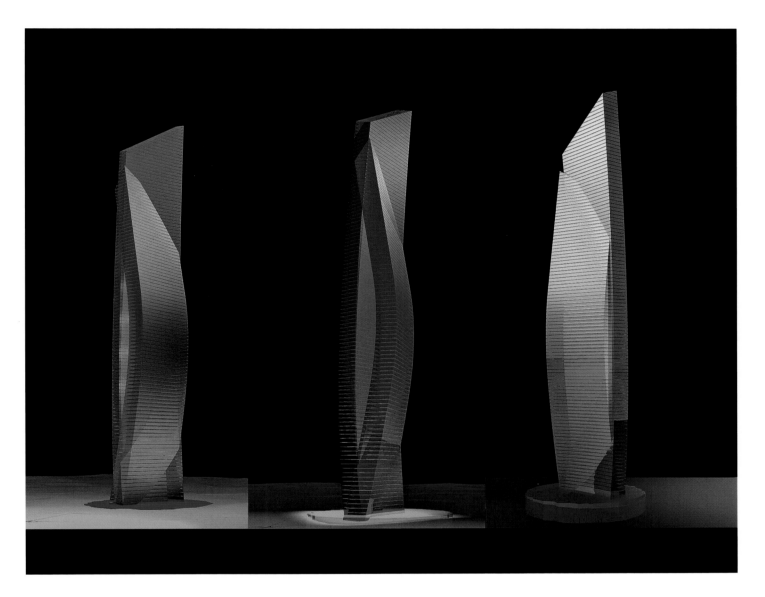

One of the alternatives for the Daewoo tower design was the pioneering Fluid High Rise. Marx's own reading of twentieth-century historical developments in architecture corresponds with Frank Lloyd Wright. The breaking of the box took place through the slide between spatial planes and rectilinear fluidity. After World War II, Le Corbusier's Ronchamp offered an emotional response to war technology through expressionist forms. The late 1990s were the stage for a renewed expression of nature. The Fluid High Rise got the endorsement of the engineering firm Ove Arup, which performed a structural analysis validating the design idea. Friends and colleagues gave varied interpretations of this project. Some called it swimmer legs in the water; others equated it to a womb. The most potent reference, according to Marx, is the building as blades of grass. Marx had envisioned a gigantic, vertically suspended garden in the interstices.

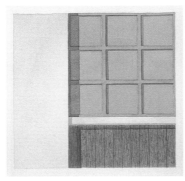

2

Scale

Architectural possibilities are found everywhere. From ordinary to extraordinary institutional projects of prominent civic presence, each commission holds a unique opportunity to inspire wonder and elation. For instance, in the hands of architects such as Arne Jacobsen, Mies van der Rohe or Smith & Williams, gas stations can turn from utilitarian real estate into destinations, even becoming the subjects of iconic photographs. The intentional content the designer carries out in the project is what differentiates the forgettable from the memorable, no matter the building type or location. Scale is the omnipresent constant—and yet also the independent variable in yielding quality in design—in such extreme ends of the building activity. All designers, talented and not, will eventually confront the change in scale from micro to macro during the crescendo of their careers. Regretfully, this figurative flight of Icarus has few survivors. A great many architects stall in either the large or the small scale. Can the jittery designs of Daniel Libeskind have a robust resolution in a single family house? Will the supremely minimalist residential visions of John Pawson have a persuasive urban correlate in the city? Has Philippe Starck truly been able to externalize in the massing and building skin the wit permeating his interiors and product designs that has generated such roaring popularity?

So far Marx has offered a smooth transition between these distant endpoints. The set of ideas and themes preceding his actual designs are traceable through these variously sized and located propositions. At the micro end of the spectrum, the romance of San Francisco informs the architectural outreach of the Beach House addition, overlooking the incomparable scene of the San Francisco Bay. At the macro end, technological ambitions in India generated the four-million-square-foot Falling Lotus Blossom complex. The thread between these opposites is a desire for place, a quest for visual excitement, and an entrenched belief in the power of geometry to produce collective bliss.

two

Falling
Lotus Blossoms _pune, india_

The almost-completed Falling Lotus Blossom compound in Mumbai, India, is the final destination in this exploration of scale change. This winning competition entry occupies a site that is part of the special economic zone established by the government to encourage development. India is the world's largest social democracy with distinct restraints on commerce. This zone is the first one based on building construction. At the competition stage the program was for two million square feet on a flat site—almost virgin land only a few years ago—overlooking a river and the fields beyond. The lotus blossom shape informed the project from the start, laid out in different iterations to see what kind of public space they would generate. Eventually Marx settled on grouping the blossoms like a clover, with a space at its heart. Heat and humidity in the country are so extreme that inhabitants do not use the outdoor space of the sunny plaza. Marx needed to collect the project together metaphorically rather than as a populated place a few months of the year. Later on, the project grew to four million square feet. Each structure increased to one million square feet, leading to the current four-building arrangement around a central void. Three atrium spaces are semi-conditioned between each of the four volumes and each of the blossom petals. This creates the kind of functional "place you want to be," in addition to the allure of the buildings themselves. Rather than affording one grand place you want to be, the project got several: the tip end of all the buildings, the little courtyard, the shapes of the buildings themselves. Even at this stage of construction, the complex already enjoys iconic status in the local community.

In addition to the sheer scale of the project, the process of its determination was innovative in and of itself. Marx conceived the project, including the site diagrams and the buildings, entirely by himself in form•Z, then saved it as a 3D Studio model and sent it to India electronically, where a local architect—the studio NPAPAL—extrapolated all the working drawings from it. Marx did not send any two-dimensional documentation. Moreover, he was minimally involved in the execution of the project. Yet the loss of architectural data in this unprecedented translation is virtually negligible: what you see in the model is what is being built.

The 21st-century workplace sets a grand scale in counterpoint to the rugged Indian countryside. Aerial views of the blossom-like forms serve as a reminder that Nature remains the inspirational source of the architecture of the future.

Raised on its own ground plane, the complex picks up a teleological dimension in becoming a quasi-temple devoted to a technical tomorrow and endowed with its iconography.

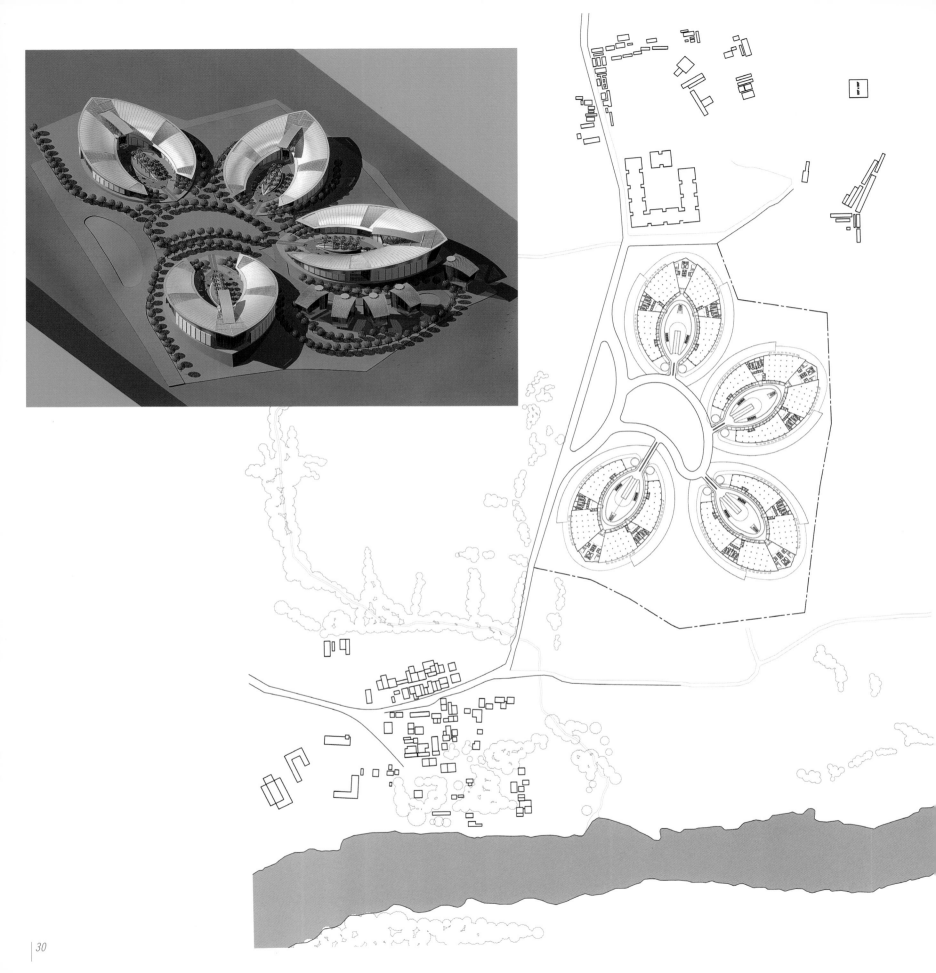

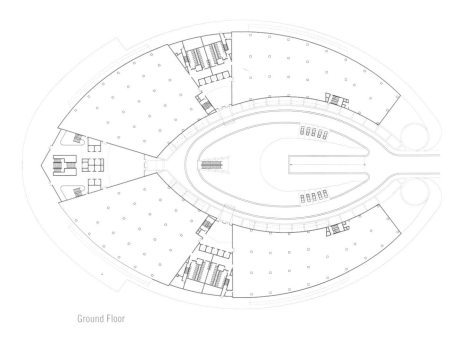

Ground Floor

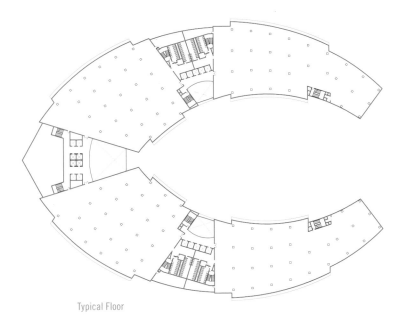

Typical Floor

As the eye follows the sweeping shape of the roof line a vivid image of the fluid plane emerges. The building opens up and embraces the users of a new society.

Marx believes that on a global scale, cultures have different energy levels for art in different periods of their existence. In his view, the American excitement for architecture as an art form died in the 1970s. Conversely, he claims that the desire to produce work of cultural significance is still active in large parts of the world. The knowledge gap between indigenous firms and the international firms has narrowed dramatically in recent years. Architecture around the world has passed the age of mimicry and has produced more and more original work. Growing economies drive these changes. Countries with greater financial resources can afford to indulge in their own cultural celebration, largely in a technology-based manner. India, China, South-East Asia, and Dubai represent such places. While they are rich in indigenous traditions, they tend to lean on Western models to give form to the aspiration of artistic currency. Past architectural models do not provide feasible references to the need of contemporary construction and technology.

To those who comment that a place like India has a rich inventory of traditional architecture, as well as a worthy heritage of Anglo-Indian provenance, and wonder at the relevance of Falling Lotus Blossom, Marx has a very clear response. Ancient and traditional Indian landmarks are not buildings that operate like contemporary structures. There is no technological precedent for a 50-story building in traditional India. Technology changes architectural reality, and what architects can do in terms of mechanical systems. Upon meeting Indian people in their own territory, they prove to be like people everywhere else: they want a better life for themselves. More often than not this equates to technological advancements in all sectors, such as a reliable electrical grid, access to clean water, and the like. They also want iPhones, color TVs, and computers. All those gadgets have no historical precedents. Marx explains it: "How would you redesign an iPhone to make it look Indian? What would that look like? Would it make sense?" It is through technology that architecture, for better or for worse, will acquire new identities as humankind ploughs through the never-ending project of life improvement.

At dusk, each courtyard morphs into a giant kaleidoscope by the delineation of building elements with neon lightning. Traveling in this hyper-reality the architectural experience keeps shifting as the night processes.

Mondrian's Window |
Beach House

san francisco, california

The San Francisco infill project, a lot narrower than the typical 25-foot parcel, only heightened the challenges of building in a city as beautiful as it is impervious to the insertion of the new, culturally and legally speaking. This slice of solid frontage along the street is graced with a tongue of landscaped terrain 100 feet long on stepped topography. Although the compression of the site did not lend itself to the curvaceous geometry typical of Marx, this flavor remained in the ceiling design of the upper floors, including the room with the most spectacular view. This addition remained invisible from the street, but would endow the existing residence with more breathing room for everyday functions. Closer to a tower in character, this appendix would accommodate the kitchen and the social spaces on the highest level, to provide entertainment. This is architecture of linearity and sequence, where all of the rooms have a sightline, progressively more expansive as one moves higher, overlooking the Bay. The rear elevation in this instance forms the primary façade, which is rich in explicit formal references. They range from the Dutch cabinet maker/architect Gerrit Rietveld for volumetric composition, to Dutch painter Piet Mondrian for the subdivision of the glazing and its coloring, and contemporary New York architect Richard Meier for the expression of frames containing the individual windows in and out of the primary building envelope. Through a language of planes, Marx hints at a much bigger scale than what the current footprint really affords. In breaking down the smaller elements, Marx avoids blatant symmetry, while simultaneously remaining elusive. As a result, there is some symmetry in the middle floor, wherein the sectional ins and outs activate the default flatness of the elevation. Selective use of dichroic glass suggests further scale as a pursuit of optical vibrancy.

View of existing house from garden.

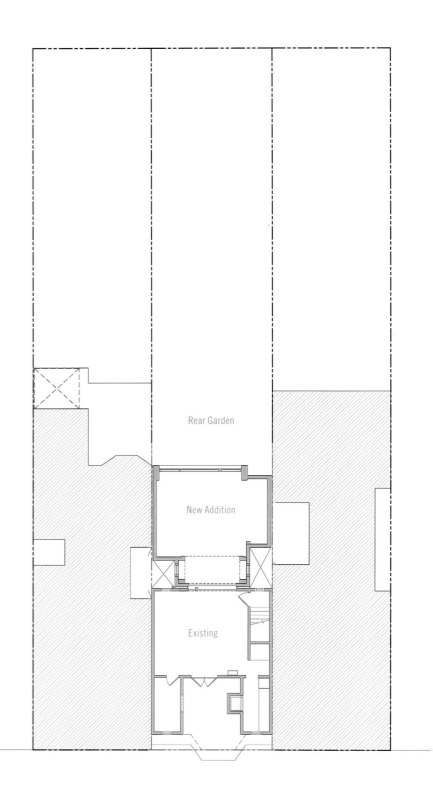

Rear Garden

New Addition

Existing

Living Room

"Empty" Room

Art Room

Existing Dining

Existing Bedroom

Existing Entrance

Existing Garage

In Roman mythology, Janus is a god with two faces one looking toward the future and the other toward the past, similarly the addition to this one-bedroom house for two artists overlooking the Bay represents a creative front where artwork is carried out, whereas the existing part allocated to routine functions faces the street.

Living Room

Dining Room

Bath-room

Kitchen

3rd Floor

Empty Room

Bedroom

Entry

Bath-room

2nd Floor

Studio

Garage

Bath-room

1st Floor

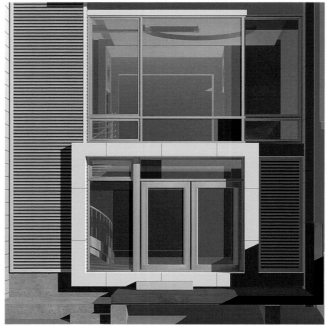

Renowned Bay Area architect William Wilson Wurster once said that in San Francisco houses are not about what you are looking into, but what you are looking out to. This giant window frame is precisely a homage to that notion.

3

Genius Loci

At its core, architecture is synonymous with place making. When the act of building results in a non-place, the metaphysical raison d'être of architecture ceases to exist. In his latest book, *Why Architecture Matters,* famed architecture critic Paul Goldberger reminds our generation of readers of a foundational lesson the great architect Louis Kahn delivered to twentieth century modernism: "A great building must begin with the immeasurable, go through measurable means when it is being designed, and in the end must be immeasurable". All landmark buildings—whether designed by signature architects or unidentified builders—are generative of place. They record history, they are repositories of remembrance, and they set the stage for the formation of new memories. Places anchor individuals and collectives to geographic particularity. They soothe pain, they trigger nostalgia and melancholia, they promote a sense of belonging and civic pride, they sponsor yearning for idealized happiness, and they provide orientation in our sense of selves. It is in places that history unfolds. And if it is true that place making is an act that involves the passage of time—the symbolism of Rome is a function of its architecture as well as of its 3,000 years of history—architecture can lend itself to enable this course. Whether stated or through mimicry, every architect endorses some idea of place through their work. Their appropriateness to the context in which they operate is met more often than not with uneven consensus, and occasionally downright contempt, depending on which circles that architectural proposition is presented for public scrutiny.

three

Purely abstracted spaces hardly make place. This conclusion that Marx reached in the course of his design itinerary is the sum of two metaphorical vectors: one biographical, the other educational. Growing up in a small town of 14,000 in Illinois, the receptive youth soon-to-be architect internalized a landscape of predictable flatness and tedious topographic character, for many being the prevailing image of the Midwest. During those early years in his impressionable mind there was a strong sense that a whole world out there full of places was to be discovered. That burning desire, so intense in his imagination, fuelled the first 22 years of his life and explains his resolve to move west to the San Francisco Bay Area, where the energy of the public realm of the city and the rich variety of its natural surroundings contribute to the magic so deeply instilled in the American imagination.

The educational vector was his exposure in college to the beginnings of environmental psychology as an acknowledged research domain and the formation of the Environmental Design Research Association, commonly known as EDRA, which is an international, interdisciplinary body, composed of design professionals and social scientists, founded in the late 1960s. Environmental psychology was one of his minors in college, and he took many courses on that subject. Reading the groundbreaking studies by famed cultural anthropologist Edward Twitchell Hall (1914-2009) proved to be a major influence on Marx's understanding of space.

Through a summer research position and under the supervision of professors in the Environmental Psychology research he undertook on a project on day care for the elderly where he wrote the about the intersection of environmental psychology and architecture. What to do with wanderlust for the elderly was the theme of that research project. Marx was the sole architect on the team working closely with a sociologist. It was an interdisciplinary approach that he has cultivated over the years and that has been driving his architecture all along. While form-making is a compelling artistic exercise, by itself it does not yield place. So what does make place?

The concept of layering so characteristic in Marx's design of building envelopes is applicable to the larger question of how architecture operates in the real world. It is a true statement that buildings have an incredibly complex layering of different things that they do and some of them do it just because they exist and through no fault of the designer. Yet he wanted to be more deliberate in that process. That involves the definition of a formal solution of the shape of the pieces that are going to define the space of the program. But how users process and experience the buildings is another matter. A classic case in point is the design of a plaza. While all the formal elements might be there, the plaza might fail to yield place, due to a lack of integration of structural features germane to the promotion of public life. Creating a workable plaza requires taking notice of those elements. Marx is deeply concerned with finding out what a great place is both from environmental psychology and design points of view.

Marx's passion for place making plays out in a number of noteworthy ways. For him, a foundational aim of design is to engender spaces of social and formal significance. Program requirements and architectural form become generative of a romantic extension of the "place you want to be". His starting points are the basic program components. Someone's office is a place, but the collection of offices together can create a place to have community. The way the architect designs the project for that user group and the spatial arrangement of its components will facilitate—or discourage—human exchange. That dynamic is going to determine the success of that facility as a cohesive bonded place where all participants are encouraged through the architecture to create relationships with each other. The architect can kill that notion with thoughtless design. Place making is the antidote to that undesirable result.

In the following assortment of projects the underpinnings of place-based design work find original architectural expression in highly diverse circumstances. With each commission radically different from one another as far as scale, location, building type, and being either private or public projects, the genuine commitment to create places informs Marx's design endeavors. It is when the walls of all these architectures start symbolically absorbing the highs and lows of being in the world, when they record in their weathering past and present human activities and those yet to come, that they become places—de facto repositories of emotional identities.

House of
Borrowed Light *san francisco, california*

The House of Borrowed Light is the most telling example of Marx's penchant for designing spaces that matter. This penthouse conceived for an affluent Asian entrepreneur splitting his time between London and the Bay Area crowns an unremarkable high rise in downtown San Francisco authored by the noted architectural firm Skidmore, Owings and Merrill during the confused years of Post-Modernism. The original layout of the skyscraper springs from an abstract grid that orders balconies, columns, duct shafts as well as fully occupied residences. This neutral box afforded an architectural experience that was neither special nor unique. That geometry had nothing to do with living. The rigidity of the modules was Marx's departure point from which to challenge the impersonal character of the tall building. The only notable feature was how the erosion of this tall building at the very top gave way to a series of balconies.

The notion of place plays out on a dual level in this project: the first is the metaphoric sense of its location in the context of San Francisco; the second is the penthouse in the context of the client's life. The pragmatics of the brief required Marx to bring light back into the north-facing residence, since the front door falls in the darkest part of the plan. This programmatic priority led to borrowing light from everywhere else in order to deliver it to the depths of the internal areas and provide an opportunity for place-making. Glass surfaces reign in the subdivision of the space and deliver privacy where needed, as well as gentle natural light. On the formal planning part of the design, Marx, working with Form4 colleague, David Perez, designed environmental themes unique to the microclimate of San Francisco, like the infamous swirling fog of the Bay Area. These metaphors drove shapes, material surfaces with etched glass, and the curving forms into spatial dialog with each other. Private and public spaces were loosely subdivided, and never rigidly enforced.

The interplay between adjacencies and relationships is the defining feature of the plan. The client wanted a space to relax with his family and friends and contemplate the natural scenery. The project is thus only partially a place for social gatherings. Had it been a social space, a different character would have been designed. Upon entering the space, the visitor faces a drum covered with a mural representing Chinese characters and images of the client's family. To the right of the drum is the private side of the space, and to the left is the public side. Yet both sides flow into one other; they quickly open up from the entrance to the public side and spill toward the kitchen and the dining area to merge into the bedroom. Everything speaks to creating a sense of place. The ceiling is an animated space-defining device designed in form•Z, not conceived in the traditional plan and elevation. Office collaborators translated the digital model into the AutoCAD files, but the iterative creative process took place in form•Z. Due to the geometric complexity of the interior space, what proved to be the most efficient use of the digital model for construction was to actually print the entire plan full scale on 55 sheets. The fluid translation from the digital file into construction was so seamless that the general contractor had no significant layout questions.

After this complete redesign, the enfilade of terraces remains the only place in the penthouse where one can read the original geometry of the building. Everywhere else, the eye is drawn into a series of curvilinear shapes. The "place to be" is the fireplace area, with the kitchen presenting a very worthy second. A cornerstone of Marx's approach to placemaking is the idea that the space has to support the lifestyle of the client it is designed for. If purely abstract, that space will not work and will lack in personality. Space has to be tailored to the client's needs, not to the architect's idealized notion of contemporary living in general. That situated-ness is prerequisite for sense of place to occur. Ideally, design is a reflection and an extension of the client's personal taste. Should this condition be fulfilled, when the clients move their objects into the space there will be a perfect fit between design and life. That is place.

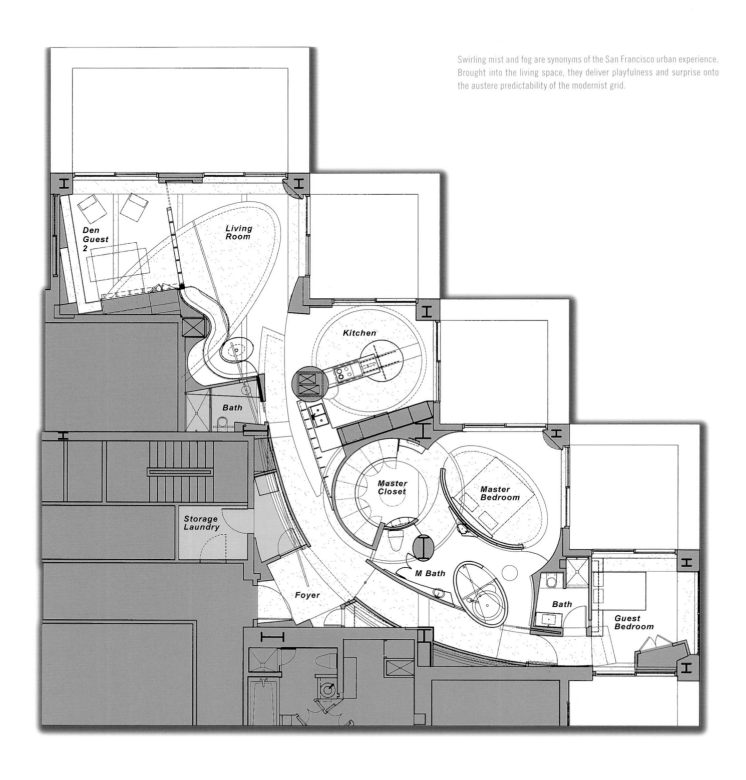

Swirling mist and fog are synonyms of the San Francisco urban experience. Brought into the living space, they deliver playfulness and surprise onto the austere predictability of the modernist grid.

Den Guest 2

Living Room

Kitchen

Bath

Master Closet

Master Bedroom

Storage Laundry

M Bath

Foyer

Bath

Guest Bedroom

Upon entering the space a multi-layered mural wrapping the drum holding the master closet gives the first imprint to the visitor. This illustration is a composite of pre-China land deeds, ancient Chinese landscape paintings and European architectural drawings on sepia-tone.

In its closed position, this enclosure is designed to be plain and sculptural, an extension of the living room. As it opens up, its true function as a kitchen is revealed.

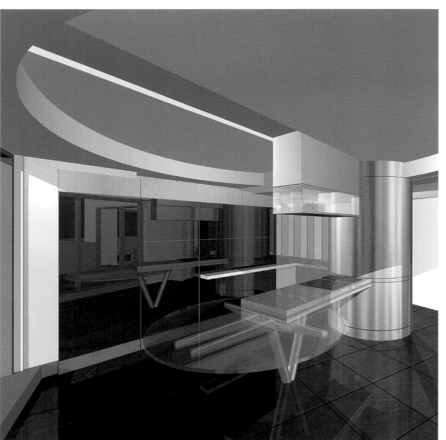

An early digital image shows the simplicity of the design intent. A large stainless steel cylinder acts as an anchoring element in the design. The cylinder hides a duct shaft which could not be moved.

The fog is architecturalized in elliptical cylinders of etched glass. Sightlines meet forms over forms, yet their luminosity remains intact.

The Ark
walnut creek, california

This conception about place-making is under constant test regardless of building type, scale, and location, and even more importantly, independent of its prominence in relation to its surroundings. It is universally applicable, but deeply qualitative in nature and therefore vulnerable to the sensibility—or lack—of the designer. The Ark, in Walnut Creek (a wealthy suburb of the San Francisco East Bay), is a transit-oriented development project. The trend toward increased density in mass transit triggered this un-built commission of a five-story building on a zero-lot-line parcel. In the project, Marx laments the emotional detachment of current modernism and the city. The search for an iconic object—contemporary, crisp, and with character—bore a distinct massing with angled roof-lines and dynamic architectural forms. The personalized rendition of a pitched roof covers this housing project where the uppermost floor is a loft space. City Council members lauded the project as exemplary for design finesse and environmental strength.

Opposite: The "place you want to be" is the destination of the architectural promenades scripted in the spatiality of John Marx. All building types have the potential for place making and for the delivery of a climax. The top floor facing the landscape is where that journey concludes.

Penthouse

Condo

Condo

Garage

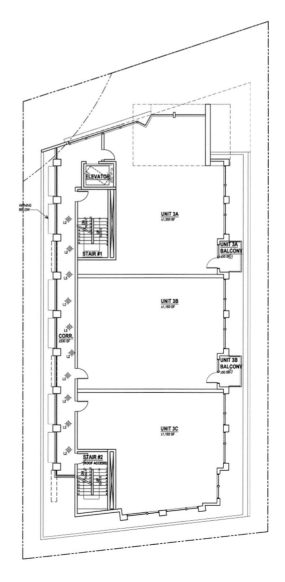

ELEVATOR

UNIT 3A
±1,360 SF

STAIR #1

UNIT 3A
BALCONY
±50 SF

UNIT 3B
±1,160 SF

CORR.
±530 SF

UNIT 3B
BALCONY
±50 SF

AWNING
BELOW

UNIT 3C
±1,160 SF

STAIR #2
(ROOF ACCESS)

Penthouse Plan

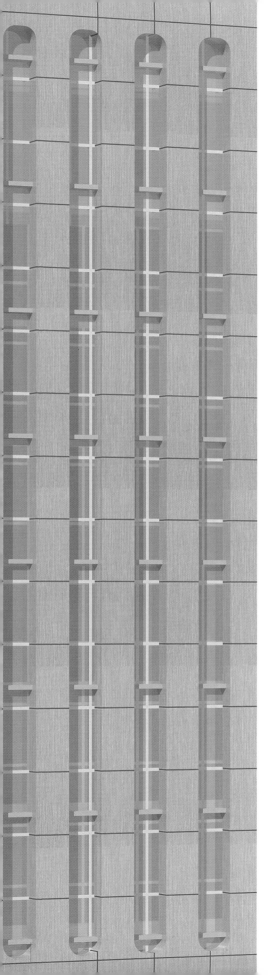

Oasis *santa clara, california*

A commission from the Silicon Valley-based Sobrato family—"The Oasis"—located on a tight urban parcel facing the Great America theme park, became an avenue for Marx's exploration of the digital form. This un-realized massing is part real, part prototypical. It is also signals the inevitable shift in higher density and transit-oriented developments that are taking place in Silicon Valley. Here Marx is after an iconic beacon that expresses innovation, design, and a sense of grace in the suburban landscape. The vertical circulation diagram is the organizing principle behind the architecture. This raised frame is 300,000 square feet and ten stories tall. It holds large floor plates and dissolves into the ground through a cylindrical glass lobby, a smaller volume for a cafeteria, and an undulating landscape, all pierced strategically to send light down into the parking garage. The Mondrian-esque skin design fixes in space an iconic balcony, the "place you want to be" for this project.

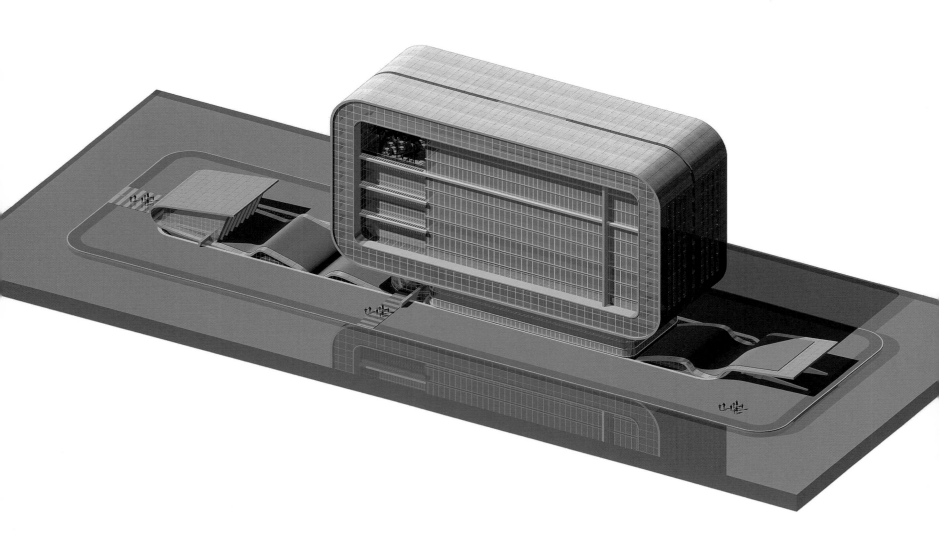

Could this be the beginning of a new iconography for Silicon Valley? To stand out as opposed to disappearing in an anonymous background is one of the regenerative powers of architecture.

Lifted in the sky, a garden and generous open space draw attention against the sleek gesture of the architectural move.

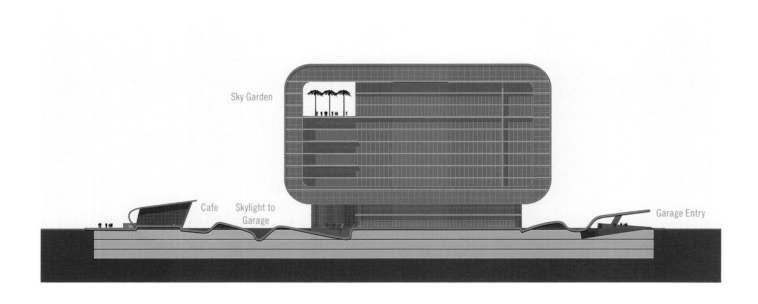

Sky Garden

Cafe

Skylight to
Garage

Garage Entry

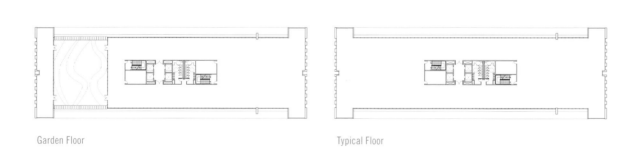

Garden Floor

Typical Floor

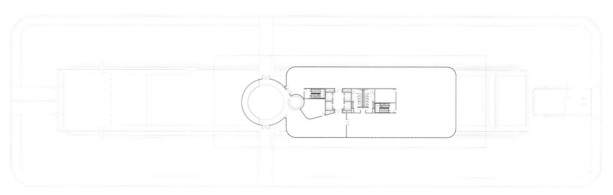

Ground Floor

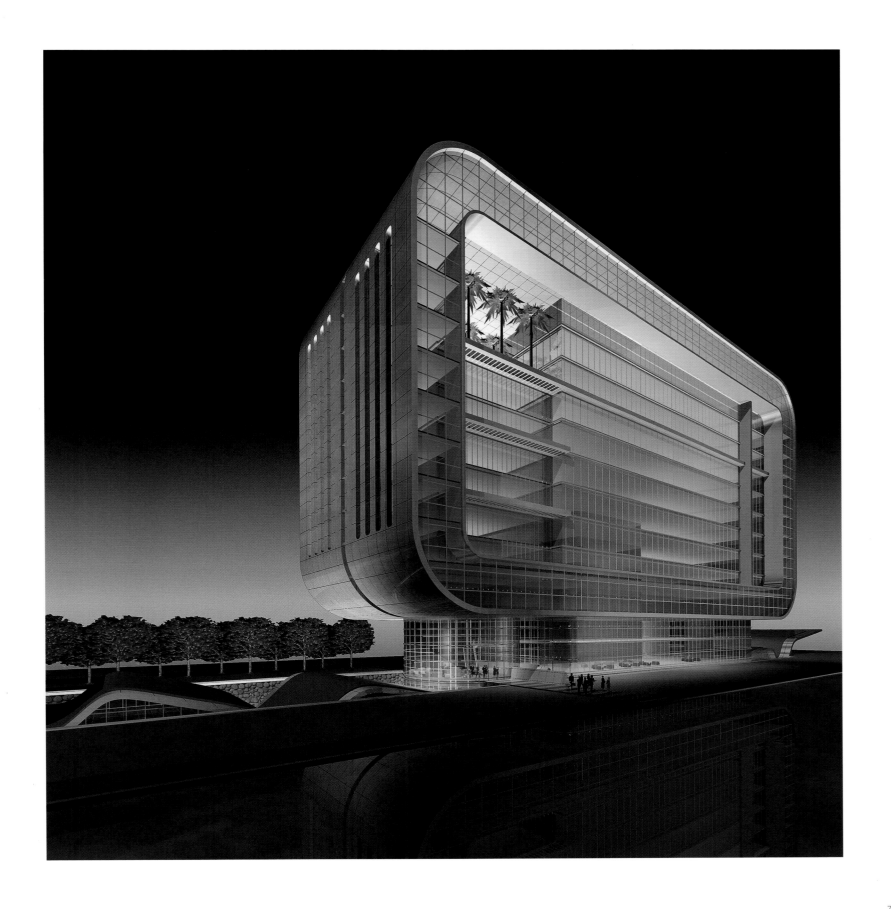

Lyrical Seashore *kaohsiung, taiwan*

Kaohsiung Maritime Cultural & Popular Music Center

If place is the locus for the dignified unfolding of the everyday and the memorable, it must necessarily transcend scale and imbue everything and everywhere with architecture. This competition entry carries out this core belief by embracing in one sweeping move a sizeable portion of the harbor of Kaohsiung, the second largest city in Taiwan, and turning it into an exercise of operating both at the level of architecture and urban design. On this overly visible tray of liminal land, Marx distributes volumes of program aimed at intensifying the urban pulse of the populace. The sensuous yet logical form of ships and the fluidity of music are the two themes Marx drew from the program and the site that set the tones for the seductive spatiality and repertoire of shapes in this ambitious scheme. The partial ring of performing art facilities interspersed with a dense network of retail and restaurant elements, as well as large cultural institutions blend into a necklace of buildings that secure human activities on a 24-hour cycle and avoid the ghost-town effect of the Sydney Opera House after hours. The existing curvilinear railway line is now used as a bicycle path, and the shape of the site itself triggers the fluid geometry of the final form. The large chunk of real estate contains a large indoor concert hall for 5,000 people and a 12,000-person outdoor performance area both placed at the center with two fingers of facilities on both sides. Facing the city, the project appears like a two-story curtain of architectural objects with giant portals functioning as public plazas to protect view corridors toward the water. The most significant of these is between the indoor and outdoor auditoria. There is a string of eight individual performance spaces with restaurants, shops and a recording studio at the tail end of the plot, caressing the more dense side of the city, which Marx envisions as a nightlife district. The opposite end is more industrial in nature and hosts the Marine Culture Exhibit Center, a music innovation center and a leaning observation tower, the complex's vertical landmark on the city skyline.

The lyrical essence of music and graceful nature of sea life are the inspirational sources for this necklace of fluid forms.

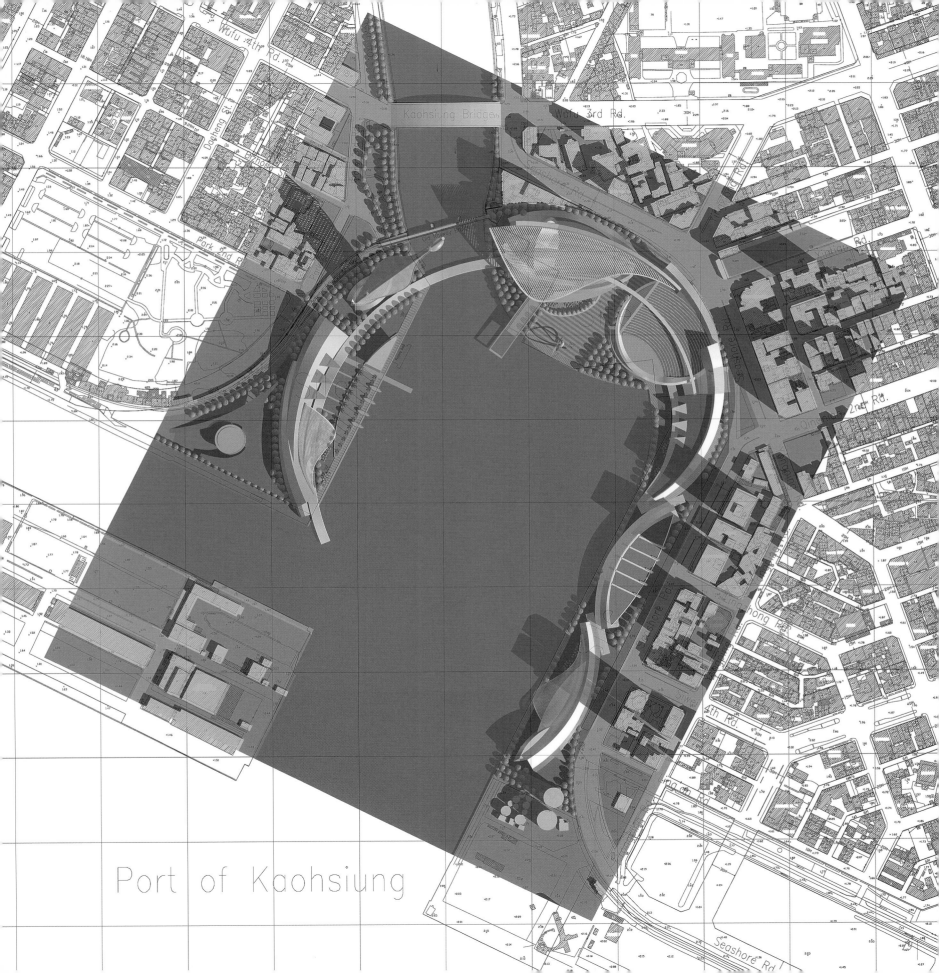

Port of Kaohsiung

The project site is prominent and liminal. Distinct formal episodes arrayed along a circuit offer a big embrace of the city.

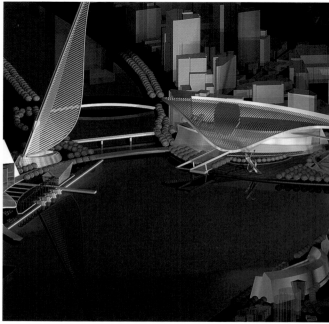

Opposite: As city dwellers approach this area they enter a grandiose urban getaway to the waterfront form the primary access road.

4

Sub / Urbane Place

The true measurable reality of built architecture since the Renaissance is the swing of the design pendulum between historicism and hypermodernity. The Renaissance marked a time when a generation of new work was a matter of interpretation, and rearrangement of classical orders from antiquity were used to give character to new building types. Since then, architects have either reached into the future or retreated into the past, depending on where the anxiety of the human condition was at the historical time in which they operated. Popular and scholarly surveys enlist landmarks embodying these collective conflicts, all of them invariably subsuming an idea of place. The fact remains that when architecture goes from the realm of the speculative to the realm of the real world, its success is entirely dependent on a binary function that only takes two arguments: place and people. Two celebrated projects representing the polarity of these two kinds of space will make such distinctions even more evident: the Piazza d'Italia in New Orleans, by American architect Charles Moore, and the Pompidou Center in Paris, France by the Pritzker Prize-winning Italian master Renzo Piano.

The former operates on a metaphoric level, drawing upon the rich architectural heritage from sixteenth-century Italy. Multiple references to those masterpieces are abstracted and reorganized here in an effort to express the iconography of a country central to the development of Western culture. This learned exercise has an eerie counterpoint in the fact that the Piazza d'Italia is actually fenced all around, desolate and deserted. Completely disconnected from the city fabric, over time it has become a token of urban abandonment, ironically so, because in Italy the piazza is synonymous with vibrant civic activity.

four

Conversely, the latter is a grand example of mechanical fantasy. Dropped in the middle of old Paris, it has a wide-open sloped plane in front and generates extraordinary vitality throughout the neighborhood. Against all odds, this infrastructural artifact, intended to take on as many permutations as technology, learning, and museum display can yield, remains a magnet of infectious élan for tourists and Parisians alike. While both projects are without doubt paramount case studies in urban sociology, the perspective of the "man of the street" conveys the sense that the Pompidou Center is the crowning achievement in modernity connecting the popular imagination with contemporary forms of living.

The soothing familiarity of the Italian piazza and the anonymity of suburban sprawl are the two endpoints on the line measuring the importance of place-making in contemporary urban design discourse. Whether as an issue of scholarly debate in Ivy League institutions, or as a subject of colloquial discussions in the layman audience, place's function as a connector of multitudes all over the world remains undisputable. Ever since the acceleration of time—resulting in the rapid commute of people and goods as well as the rise of instant communication technologies—the Industrial Revolution has caused urban planners and theorists to formulate numerous, if often conflicting, models on how to spatially synthesize the social program of the city with the particularity of their geographical and cultural position in relation to the world. New Urbanism offers a retreat into the urban picturesque as a treatment for the alienating landscapes that modern architecture has created, based exclusively on planning principles. Star-urbanist Rem Koolhaas proposes an aesthetic of dispersion peppered with digitally styled architectural landmarks in order to give form to the present human condition. Reliance on the flagship building to regenerate city life is another answer that Frank Gehry presented in Bilbao.

In California grounds, Universal Studios in Hollywood, the Third Street Promenade in Santa Monica, and Fourth Street in Berkeley offer three obvious examples of how pedestrians connect to the built environment based on distinct forms of urbanity. In all of them, the presence of people is integral to the architecture. The urban vernacular frames these public spaces, which burst with activity, enhance human exchange, and elicit contact between strollers. Contemporary architects face this dilemma between their love affair with the heroic period of modern architecture of the 1920s and 1930s and the unintended effects of the modernization of the city under ruthless speculative forces.

To add to the aforementioned predicament, architects have a presence on the world stage. Commissions are available in remote parts of the planet. A workforce that rarely leaves the office and develops a limited perception of the condition in corners of the globe rarely visited. To practice in the San Francisco Bay Area today implies reaching beyond the immediate professional context of where the architect operates. Through that ubiquitous communication technology, the Internet, what was not too long ago the privileged purview of large corporate entities, is now readily available to mid and small-size firms equipped with current hardware and software. In 1958, Japanese architect

Kenzo Tange had already identified communication as the arena for the greatest revolution of the future in an interview with architectural writer John Peter for the landmark book *The Oral History of Modern Architecture*. Nothing could be more true fifty years after those statements were made. The results are found everywhere in one global community irrespective of political, economic and cultural boundaries. While this is a phenomenon taking place worldwide, throughout its relatively short history San Francisco has been an outpost of cosmopolitan exchange.

A sizeable portion of Marx's designs precisely engage the remote. Korea, China, India, and Brazil all pose their distinct challenges in terms of cultural backgrounds, physical settings, user groups, local building technologies, and symbolism. It comes as no surprise that interventions in these unfamiliar environments still carry elements of urban experimentation. The conundrum is how to fuse a coherent design vision of the region with any aspiration for technological advancement regardless of where it comes from. Any proposition about the future brings about fears of environmental alienation in the local community. How does the architect respond to this? What kind of cultural responses can the architect come up with? Marx takes this challenge head-on with projects imposing in scale and generative of additional modes of living, whether for the workplace, urban expressions of consumer culture, or housing. While none of these designs have definite attributes within themselves, they all stand as meeting points of the themes unique to Marx's design sensibility and the contextual pressures of each site, when, more often than not, nature, as opposed to the immediate built surroundings, become an inspirational source for his architecture. Marx also implements various strategies with distinct commonalities in his search of place in the uncomfortable social remoteness of Silicon Valley, a land known as much for its technological miracles as its estrangement, for being an undetermined tapestry for the companies of the digital empire.

In all of the projects, the common desire is to create a sense of place. Their cultural context is fractured by the contradictions of a society straddling a traditional way of thinking and the embrace of the western paradigm. To those who object to the modernization of a historically rich place like India, from an architectural standpoint that rich cultural fabric engages a technology that is no longer applicable for different scales and building systems. In the case of India, the pre-British technology is rural and based on masonry construction. If you have to design a 20-story building, there are no architectural precedents of technology that are indigenous to that community that can also support that design. Hence that culture has to engage the forces of modernization. Nonetheless the question needs to be asked: How do you tame technology and create something place-based? The "iconic" is a category diligently pursued throughout the body of work. It embodies the making of the dominant image against the skyline that lures the urban dwellers in Marx's projects and invites them into a tantalizing scenography. Another theme of his work is the layering of fluid forms, ordered in grand gestures that invariably extend beyond the site where his architecture sits. In addition, the calibrated management of open spaces in relation to the ground floor edges is an ongoing concern in a great many of his proposals. But maybe what reigns supreme is his quest for the serendipitous blend of identity and pleasure, captured in a world of architecture that citizens can place themselves into.

Serpentine Connection
nVidia Headquarters
santa clara, california

This pursuit is the undercurrent for the design of the head-quarters for nVidia, a groundbreaking business in visual computing technologies. What started as a speculative operation to develop office space for the initial clients, the Sobratos, an Italian family of entrepreneurs with large amounts of real estate in the area, became a prototype for workflows and renewed social relationships for the staff. The project is based on very tight site parameters in terms of parking requirements, producing an end result of a restricted perimeter landscape between the buildings and the surrounding parking area. The pinwheel plan spins off from its center where a public space is located. For efficiency's sake this village of buildings, with a landscape area at its core, is made of largely identical volumes, but each displays variations in façades and angles. Only one side of the floor plates is curved. The other three sides had to be rectilinear, forming a hybrid ship. Together with a sense of flow, streamlining, and dynamism of the horizontal, the green granite fins at the building's ends suggest the bow and stern of a vessel, a formal reference tied to the client's nautical interest, much to the excitement of the Sobratos.

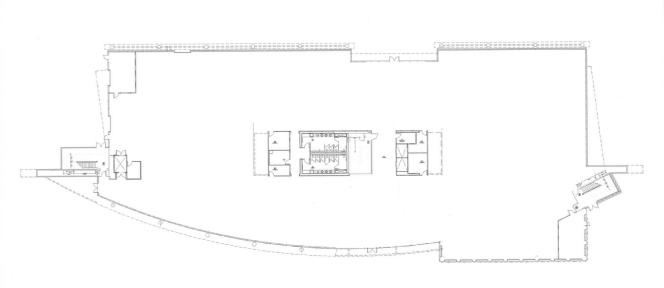

As the project was being developed, nVidia stepped in to lease the campus. This changed the primary image of the project. The need to link the buildings through bridges became the predominant goal, and the resulting bridge was informally named "the squiggle." The tenant was willing to finance the costly bridging because it became wildly popular as a place for visioning and brainstorming. The squiggle is at the upper level with restricted access. It has become a de facto outdoor office space where the workforce holds casual meetings and exchanges vital information for the creative relevance of the company. Process-wise, Marx focused on the building massing, whereas his principle colleague, Paul Ferro, worked independently on the elevations. They both presented their work to the client, who liked both results and asked to fuse the two together. The form•Z model became the interface between these heterogeneous ideas, and was traded back and forth between the two of them in a very fluid manner. Typically, Marx presents the client with an image that sells the building aesthetic, not the concept. Through these striking views, carefully crafted with digital technology, he is able to create an emotional bond with the client that lasts for the rest of the project. By showing them a range of options for the project, as opposed to one idea at a time, he builds trust, to the benefit of the project quality. In a testament to his experience, clients often pick the option he prefers.

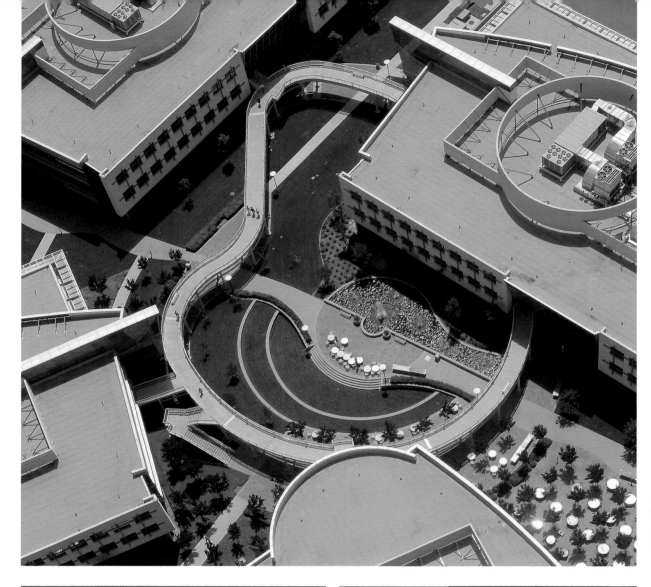

When the surroundings lack a sense of place, as in the case of virtually all Silicon Valley office parks, place-making becomes an inside-out design affair. It is the center of the project with controlled elevations and ground conditions that becomes the starting point to instilling in the users a sense of belonging.

Just like in cities, cafes are an effective trigger for urban energy and community development.

Café Culture *sao paulo, brazil*
VIOL Headquarters

In Marx's Viol competition entry in Sao Paulo, Brazil, designed in collaboration with KMD, the architect confronts a population-density issue very similar to that of Beijing. A sea of buildings and 20-story concrete towers surround a very uninviting site bounded by a Brazilian version of a freeway. Helicopter views depict the vastness of the land, unfolding a seemingly endless carpet of tall buildings. Viol asked to retrofit an existing tower and design two brand new towers for office space sitting on a two-story podium housing a retail center. "Two of the same thing creates a powerful axis and drama," Marx comments. Two towers frame the most visible corner of the site to signal the gate to the interior complex. Two smaller towers, accessible at a pedestrian level, are located at the back of the site. This urban plaza scoops you in and, despite its exposure to the highly trafficked thoroughfare, it is designed as "the place you want to be" together with the termination of the tallest towers.

While this vision does not carry the fluid character that defines so much of Marx's architecture, fluidity remains in the plan. The plaza and the public spaces are open in order to welcome pedestrian activity and promote community.

Opposite: Raising the horizon is a classic move to create a focal point in the architecture from the outside in. Unsurprisingly, here two sky gardens are the "place to be" and form an urban gate facing the city.

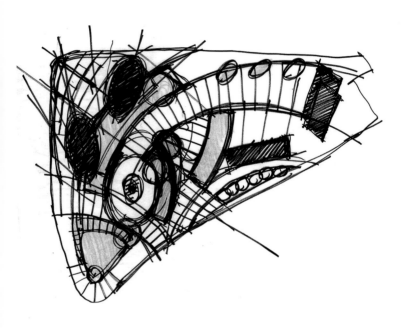

A cafe plaza and a theater bring life to the ground
level permeable to energy of the city.

Reflective Aspiration *san jose, california*
Technology Drive

The proposal for Technology Drive is an additional permutation of the chess pieces—office building, parking garage, retail component and open areas. Soft and hardscape give character to this arrangement and determine place. As the area grows in density, most of the buildings increase in height to ten stories, a limit that the airport authority has imposed on construction to protect the flight path of traffic in and out of the San Jose airport where the site is located. Positioned at the intersection of several transportation systems-the lot is near the freeway, the bus system, and to where the light rail will connect with the airport—this area lends itself to being an architectural lab to prompt yet another kind of urban living, where the individual and vehicular scales find peaceful resolution. With parking accommodation being the constant limitation in land use, the developer commissioned a design to be leased and identified as headquarters for two tenants in the same building, one lessee or even multiple tenants. This programmatic requirement shaped the core diagram and double lobby arrangement. Due to the high water table and ongoing, escalating construction costs, the option of an underground parking structure was unfeasible from the start. Therefore, parking was pushed to the back of the site and the building elements were brought out to the front edge, part of an intense effort to activate the pedestrian experience along Skyport and Technology Drives. The establishment of the urban pedestrian edge starts from the parking lot, with retail at its base, and continues along the vehicular arteries to find its climax at the corner. The already-generous sidewalk increases in width as visitors reach the corner plaza, where it is furnished with café tables and other amenities that define a more localized urban experience. A water feature, a landscape element with trees on it and the imposing cantilever of the building is reminiscent of the heroic overhangs of the Modernist cliff-hangers of California and give the space its distinctive character. The serpentine base expands and contracts in relation to the edges of the sidewalk in order to activate zones for pedestrians, who can easily occupy them in solitude or in groups. The hovering of the office tower on the plaza dramatizes the building's presence at the street corner with a long shadow that gives respite from the weather and protection from the busy vehicular thoroughfare. The wave motif informs the metaphorical eye of the building on the upper floor, where it takes on the quality of a logo for the architecture itself.

Distinction is what every company is after to assert itself in the marketplace. Architecture conjures up images that are long lasting even in those who occupy urban environments in a state of distraction. The balcony here presents a formal exception in the curtain wall system triggering awe and anticipation.

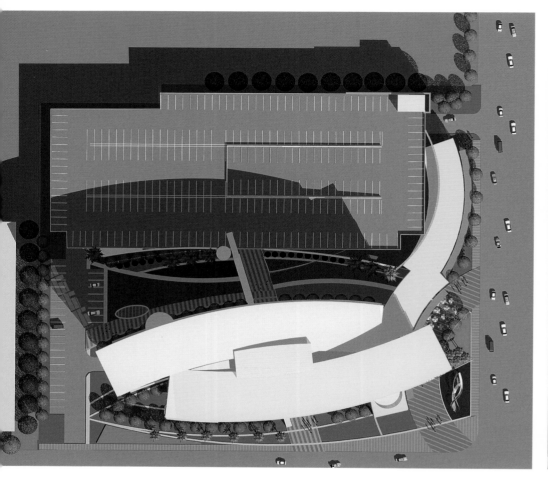

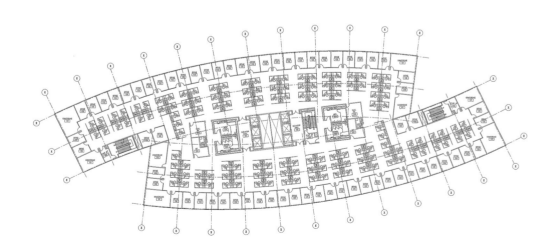

Opposite: Two-story retail base conceals parking from pedestrians.

Urban corners are solid and foundational in the city experience in Europe, but are empty in modern sprawl. This corner relies on retail and hospitality anchors to promote pedestrian participation in the public life.

Sanctuary Apex _mumbai, india_
Bradbury

With the Bradbury complex in downtown Mumbai, India, Marx fine-tunes his place-making tactic to the cultural conditions of an environment where public space is not as integrated as it is in the United States. In India, projects to this end routinely become home encampments. To mediate these unique socio-cultural conditions with the private interests of the developer, the project features an inner and outer urban space. The inner space is the heart of the project, fully activated with the program and with a grand plaza in the shade. For this gargantuan mixed-use compound, which includes a hotel and offices, the architect envisioned a small citadel brought to urban order by a large, arching street. Despite the machine aesthetic, the iconic nature of the office tower and the hotel define the dominant image of the place.

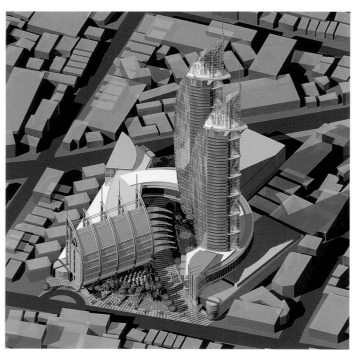

Sky Garden

Condos

Offices

Offices

Parking   Retail

Retail   Parking

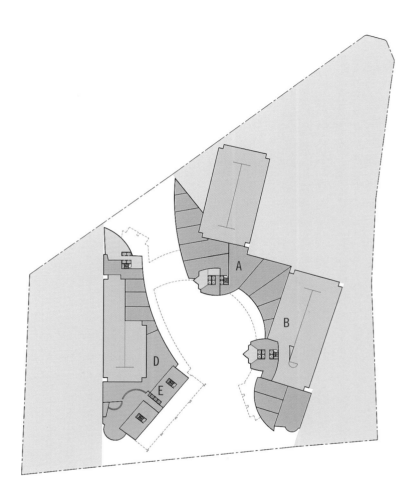

A. Retail
B. Parking
C. Office
D. Hotel
E. Restaurant

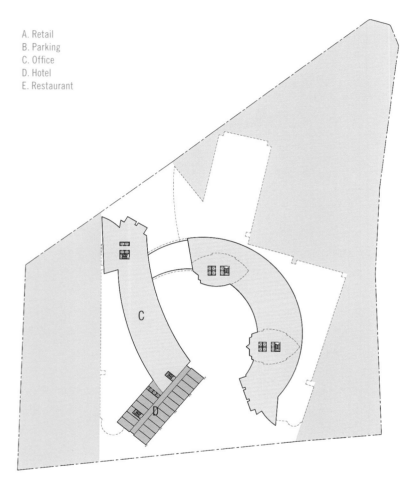

Orchestration of shapes is the theatrical ingredient for the consumption of architecture. Their stage presence is pronounced against the local skyline. Drawn in through calibrated openings toward the city fabric, visitors enter a sheltered plaza filled with retail edges and cafe amenities. Sky gardens top off this elegant pair of high rises.

Suburban Canyon *santa clara, california*
GA Campus

Place-making challenges prevail in Silicon Valley, where a vague suburbia seems to be the only outward manifestation of the cradle of the Digital Revolution. Marx pondered how to generate excitement in the architectural generics of office space, knowing that tenants routinely yearn for some design differentiation from their competitors. To tempt clients away from what is ordinarily done, Marx produces multiple options through imaginative computer modeling, increasing the chance of stepping out of the anonymity of the sprawl. The "suburban canyon" master-plan and winning entry of an invited competition takes head-on this test and promotes architectural identity through a pair of elliptical towers nested into a highly formalized hardscape, also one of Marx's signatures. This duet of waffle cone buildings aims to reshape the flat suburban skyline. A vast garage with a landscaped roof faces the towers and becomes the other edge of an internal street/park of public use. The project wants to succeed as a generator of place at an iconic level and at an urban level. Located in a region where the population is projected to grow to a million people, the area is a gateway to Silicon Valley. Prominent views from the 101 Freeway make this intervention a highlight in the bleak landscape of a place that is yet to happen in California's urban history.

Long and narrow sites close to the freeway are often leftovers with minimal chance of architectural redemption—sound and air pollution being just two of the stigmas. In subdividing the site in even thinner slices, the middle partitions turned into a canyon endowed with interwoven spaces rich in interests for pedestrians.

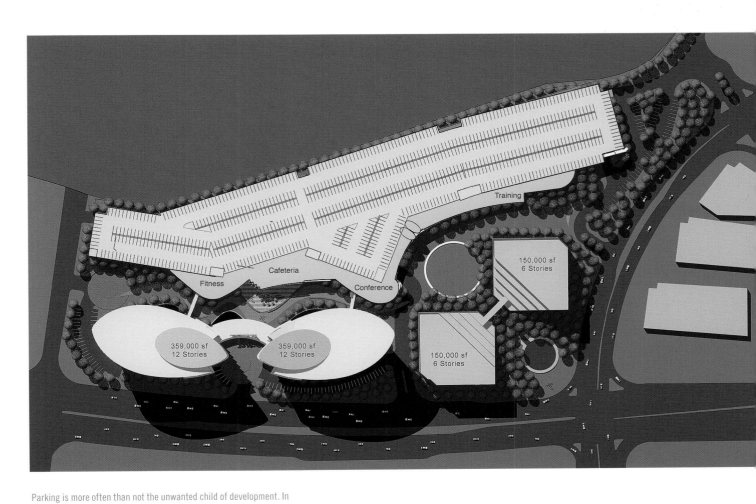

Parking is more often than not the unwanted child of development. In this case, both its rooftop and its inner edges are transformed into amenities of collective enjoyment.

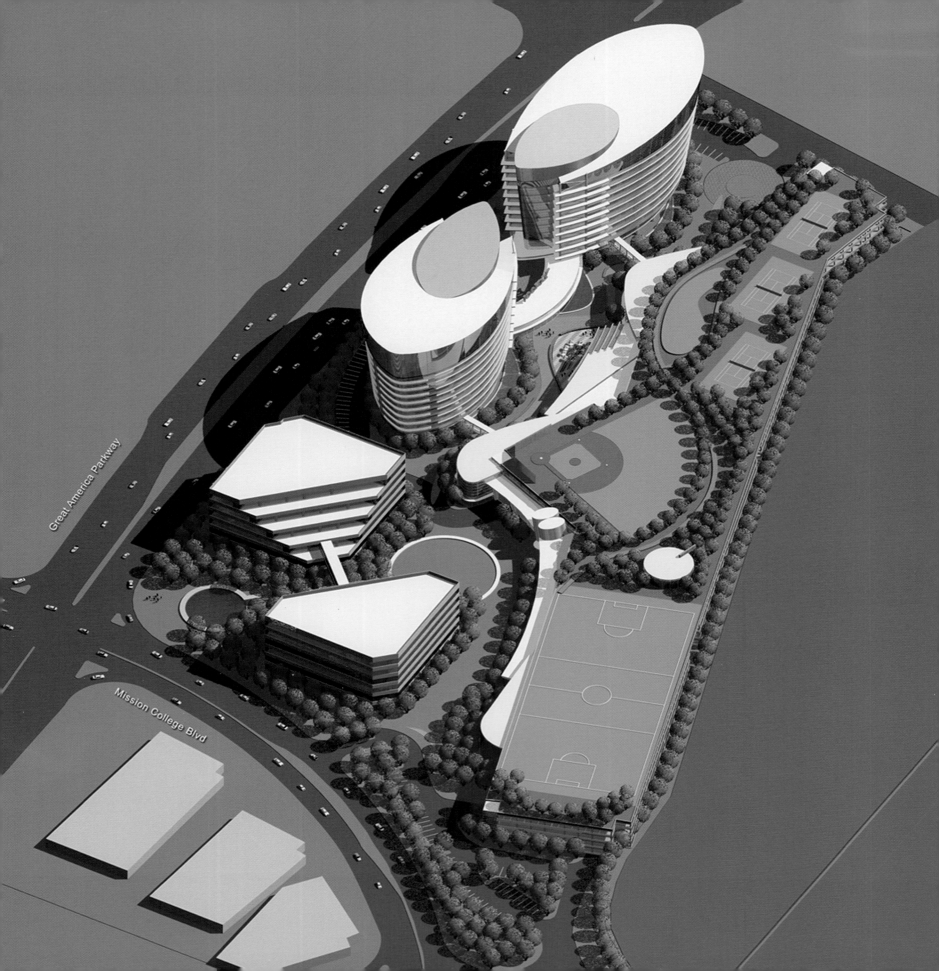

Great America Parkway

Mission College Blvd

River's Edge *mumbai, india*
Metroplex

The Metroplex design for Mumbai, India, raised entirely different concerns. In the genealogy of Indian projects that Marx authored, this adventure came after the pure geometry of the Falling Lotus Blossom compound, now almost complete. This later, developer-driven project was intended for a site on the northwest edge of the Indian metropolis of 17 million people. Wedged between a highly developed area and a wide river, the scheme aims to bring the architecture into the defining features of its surroundings. For Marx, this mixed-used multiplex reads as "a set of rivers within the site boundaries," literally an architectural translation of the neighboring natural landscape within the project boundaries. The program brief also called for four condominium towers and two hotel lobbies. Department stores, mixed use, retail, cinema, food courts, entertainment center, and video arcades are the anchors activating the space and bringing people in. The design ambition is based on the idea that once inside the architectural enclosure, one will recognize a sense of place.

Currently, the existing shopping pattern in India is based on the disorderly groupings along vehicular thoroughfares of countless individually-owned tiny stores, each with its own signage fighting for the attention of the distracted buyer. While the bustle of street life and transactions may be endearing to the tourists eye, as a commercial model it shapes commerce in ways that inhibit long-term growth, while giving virtually no foreign companies a chance to compete in the domestic market. The introduction of the American shopping (mall) into Indian territory, (ironically, the invention of the Austrian-born and Los Angeles-based Victor Gruen) puts the process of modernization of this venerable society has started on a fast track, and supplies the Indian consumer with working alternatives. This cascade of functions is structured around a meandering path with architectural solids swirling around it. This microcosm of urban experiences sits on a mostly underground parking lot with one above-grade parking level. Artfully arranged through constriction and release along the path, a new skyline emerges. For Marx, formal planning is a balancing act between boredom and fuzziness. Mystery is gone on a straight path, and the push and pull of the medieval city is a much more handy reference in the pursuit of the urban picturesque. A promenade along the river will be developed by the city to soften the transition between the Metroplex and the river. The common denominators of Marx's urban schemes are shapes in context and contest with one another. While fascinated by form, he remains aware that architecture is not a piece of sculpture and that the architect must address the issue of inhabitability. For Marx, renowned architect Frank Gehry artfully succeeds in this. The big question remains: how do you take a form that is non-rectilinear and make it habitable?

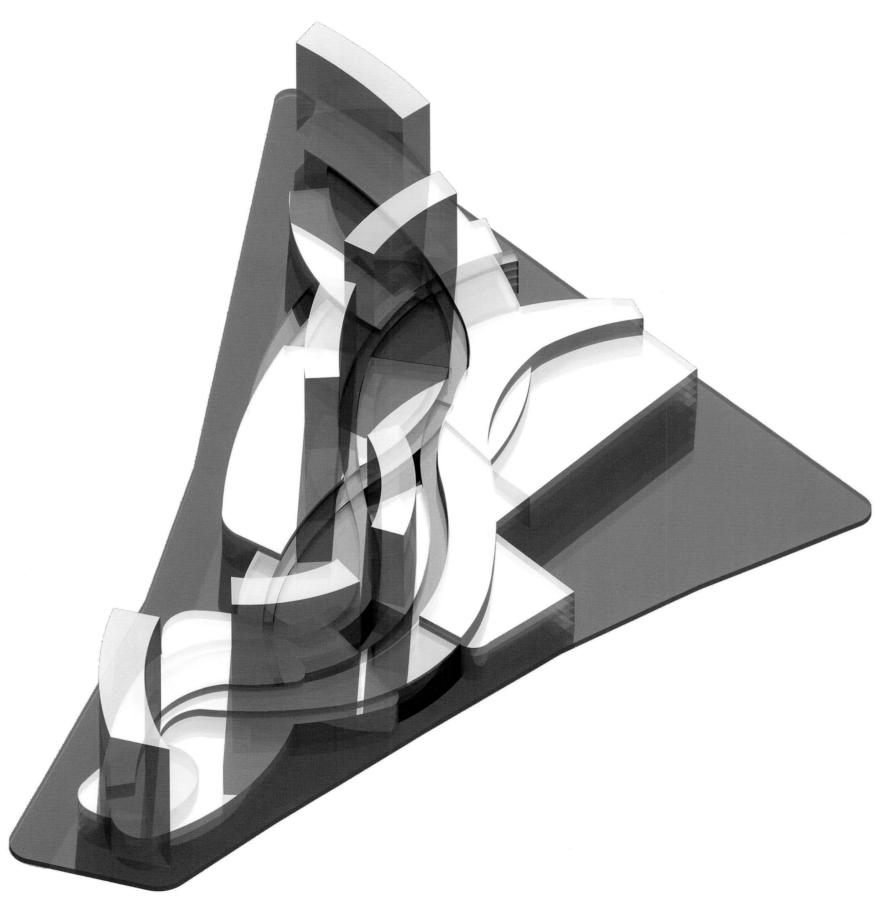

A   Hotel Tower
A1   Hotel Support
B   Residential Tower
C   Retail
D   Restaurant Zone Upper Level
E   Cinema Zone Upper Level
F   Parking Garage
G   Restaurants Ground Level
H   Atrium-Interior Open Space

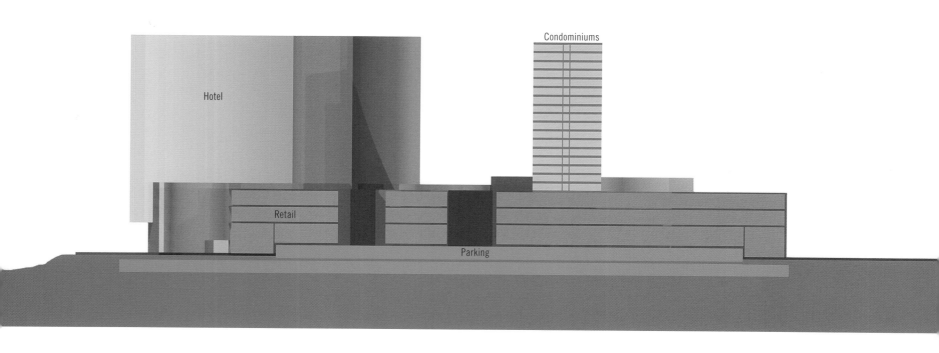

Toward the riverfront, round forms and lush gardens
frame the character of an active promenade.

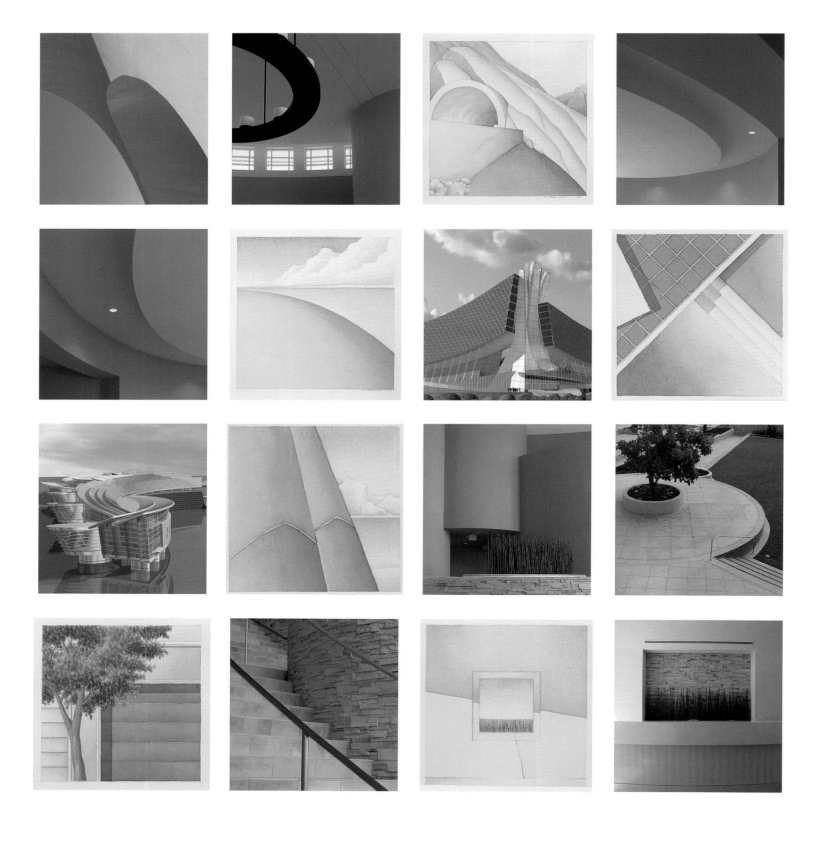

5

Materiality

Architecture is anthropomorphic by definition. This is as true a statement today as it was yesterday and as it will be tomorrow. Rather than the literal allusion to human forms that was so central to Renaissance architects, Marx's most cogent reference is to human attributes. Four out of the five senses (can architecture be tasted?) are thoroughly intertwined in the production and consumption of architectural space. Our sense of the sublime will only emerge when the scale of our body can measure itself against the magnitude of the artifacts we inhabit. Architecture loses its right to exist once it no longer serves a function for humankind, whether symbolic, utilitarian, economic, or anthropological. When that happens, it turns into an archeological ruin at best, and into a pile of materials to be recycled at worst. Human presence is integral to the endorsement of a design, irrespective of where that project ranks in discourse, whether it is the Cathedral of Chartres or a bicycle shed, to quote architectural historian Nikolaus Pevsner. The Ronchamp Chapel requires the visitor to have an experience of ineffable space, as Le Corbusier writes, in order to come into existence. And yet, in the last fifteen years, the trumpet of Web connectivity has been played so loudly that this basic understanding of architecture has been either forgotten or put into question, even when the leap from great-looking designs on-screen to the materiality of the external world has produced qualitatively intermittent results.

In his Charles Eliot Norton lectures of 1958-59, eminent classical composer Carlos Chavez argues that, besides the five senses humans are born with, there exists an aesthetic one that all humans share. He explains that this sense subsumes musical, plastic, literary, and any other artistic dimensions. Such sense —possibly an intuitive judgment, beyond language and text—is what makes both producers and consumers agree on an outcome that will transcend the contingency of any particular situation to reach renewed existential fulfillment. This operates in architecture as well. In fact, it is the searchlight that designers turn on in their explorations to embody the idealism that feeds architecture into built form. The Cartesian split between the body and the mind is reconciled into the bliss of the architectural experience.

five

Portal to the Wind *jeju island, south korea*
Jeju International Airport

"What is more global than an airport?" Marx quips when explaining his entry for the international terminal addition to a preexisting facility for the invited Jeju Island competition in Korea. Limited architectural contests in that country are fairly compensated design maelstroms—metaphorically speaking—win-or-lose. And coming up with a strong conceptual idea is critical for the Korean client. Operational obstacles at times include language translation, occasional lack of feedback, and the inevitable mediated communications through video conferencing, File-Transfer-Protocol sites, and e-mail, which more and more frequently allow designers to vicariously experience the site and have contact with clients and their representatives. Marx would argue, however, that the direct personal access in face-to-face meetings is still the irreplaceable vehicle for establishing trust and understanding in client-architect relationships.

In the Jeju proposal, the immediate material environs were constituted by an unwelcoming sea of parking against the relentless flatness of the topography, which made the scheme virtually a stand-alone building. The inspirational trigger had to spring from somewhere else. Jeju, Marx found out, is a highly sought after honeymoon spot in Korea. The original settlements constituted a fishing base, notoriously known for severe winds and a rocky coastline. Traditionally, the population listed more women than men, a sad premium to pay as their spouses lost their lives in the process of fishing the ocean. Architecturalizing the wind became the underlying formal principle of this project. The inscription of the natural element is carried out from the massing of the complex all the way through to the shape of the canopies to the circulation of the staff and the travelers. Having the wind as the form-giver for the scheme determined the curvilinear geometry that is something of a trademark in Marx's architecture. Abstracted wind currents sculpt the interior and the exterior in the tripartite layout of the project. The ramp to reach the entry point of the terminal, with its stream of vehicles and traffic to the airport, makes up the first portion. The wings at the edges of the ramp stretch the building horizontally to express the flow of the users and make up the second part. The third part includes slanted cylindrical volumes that hold the passengers before they embark on their airplanes, situated along the rounded plan. They also stand for local rocks and stones and are meant to suggest the coastline. Because the departure gates are very high, the entire airport is raised in order to use the lower level freely.

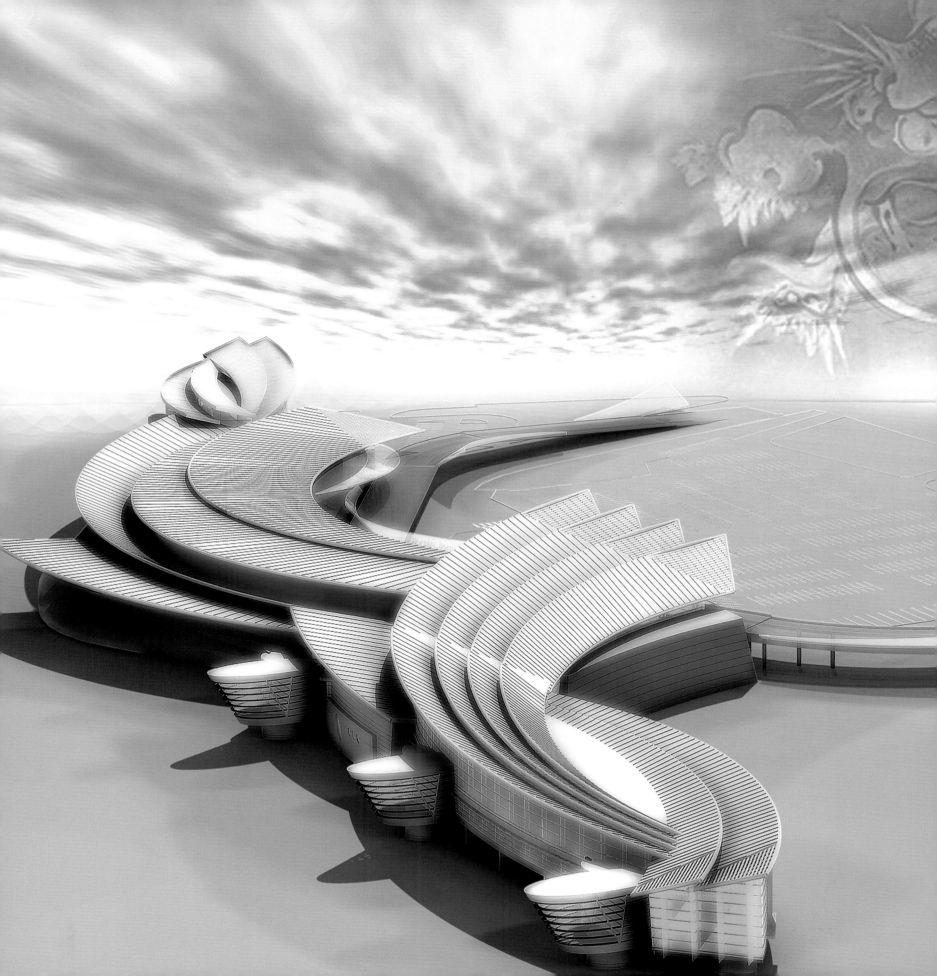

The curved geometry resulting from the existing ramp accommodating a car's turning radius gets amplified in this project to become generative of its own flowing space. Echoing the trajectory of the local winds, the ample curves of the overlapping roots yield a "regional" image to travelers.

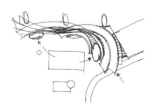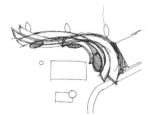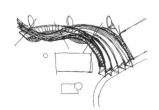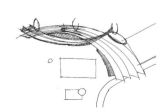

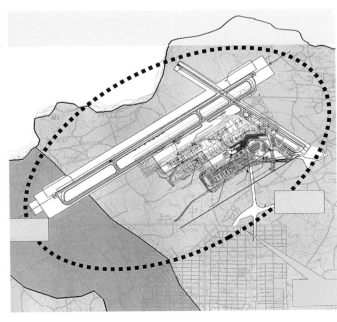

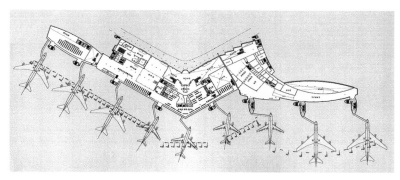

Arrival Level

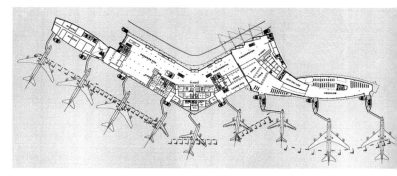

Departure Level

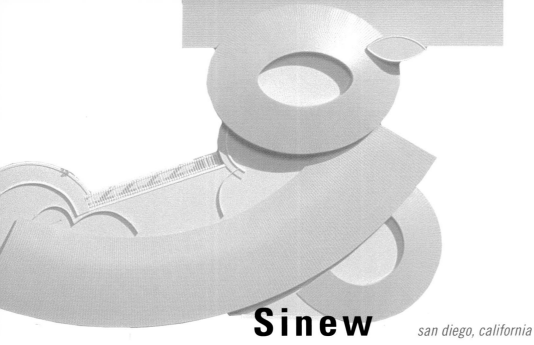

Sinew *san diego, california*
Carmel Valley Athletic Club

Marx's ideological embrace of the digital design process undergoes ongoing sensorial tests when faced with the reality of construction and the psychology of expectations. A number of his design endeavors literally deal with bringing pleasure and comfort to the body, with the dual goals of nurturing wellness and promoting social cohesion. The Pacific Athletic Club in San Diego showcases these ambitions toward material presence. Private enterprises are the up-to-date shapes of American architecture patronage. Never abandoning the relentless pursuit of their business goals, the client is nationally known for branding a form of collective fitness by offering environments that enable social interaction and feelings of relaxation in the membership. The design theme follows the idea of a resort hotel without rooms, from site plan to material selections. The complex, flirting with the idiom of the Mediterranean vernacular, is a shell for human happenings and the development of positive memories, all of which lead to an anxiety-free place. Since the feedback Marx has received relays that there are almost no cancellations once visitors join the club, the intangibility of the concept has clearly resonated with club members.

A carefully choreographed assembly of suave forms rests on a flat site with an abrupt 15-foot grade change. Visitors drive axially down a lushly landscaped boulevard toward the entrance ending in a foreground plaza. The abstracted bell tower serves as a vertical landmark and draws visitors to the main threshold punctured on an elliptical volume. Upon entering, visitors become participants of a grand architectural interior featuring a double-height lobby and an orchestrated display of convex/concave silhouettes, all functionally driven and remarkably consistent with the design language that informs the exterior. The eye is invited to scan the interior surfaces and expand its sightlines to the mountains afar. From the plan to the fittings, all elements conjure a unified design statement.

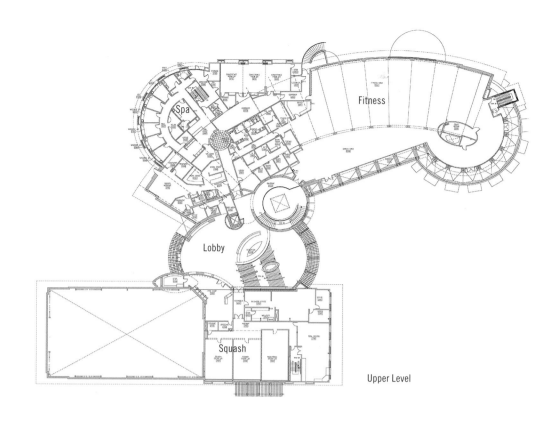

Spa

Fitness

Lobby

Squash

Upper Level

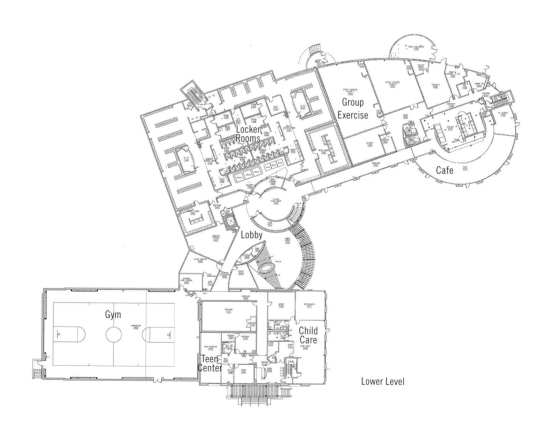

Group
Exercise

Locker
Rooms

Cafe

Lobby

Gym

Child
Care

Teen
Center

Lower Level

Long before this practice became routine, an early digital design was prepared for the client. The project was built virtually unaltered.

A variety of social spaces, dramatically different from spot to spot, are layered on a circuit. Architectural episodes activate the various programmatic areas, each with its own promise of aesthetic excitement. The building masks the view that is revealed once inside. The progression of spaces is triggered from there. A vast, sensuous void inside the round form greets newcomers. From there, guests look out to the view of the pool decks and the mountains, and the space expands toward the vistas. These forms conspire to sweep people down. Once at the lower level the space spills out onto a great lawn whose focal point is a big tree in a round disk—a gathering destination in its own right. The highly formalized open areas pour onto gentle level changes and delineate distinct sectors for communal exchange. The gym, which is half underground, half above, pulls you over and connects you with the outdoor areas furnished with amenities and various sized pools, all to promote outdoor living.

The prominent interior designer Orlando Diaz-Azcuy designed the round lights in the lobby and picked the Solan Hoffen limestone to confer a centrifugal trait to the sensuous interplay of the cylinders, which all point toward the majestic staircase. He also suggested tone and color palette within the architectural enclosure. Everything is conceived to have a relationship with the outside. From the top entry level, to the downstairs areas where the gym is positioned, to the connecting corridors looking outward, the complex continually looks to nature as the constant of the architectural experience.

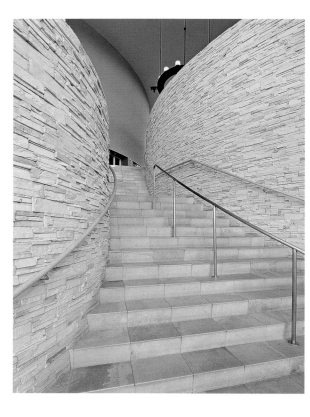

Venetian Glass
los gatos, california

Netflix Bridge

Thirty miles away from the nVidia site, in the town of Los Gatos, Marx designed the head office for Netflix, the DVD rental giant whose presence is evenly distributed in all American households. While the client chose abstracted Tuscan to mesh with the urban fabric and to comply with city planning restrictions, its interiors remained starkly contemporary. An un-built proposal for a slick high-tech bridge excited the client, but eventually a more conservative option was realized. That early idea was predicated on a contrast of styles: a clad-in-glass bridge reminiscent of a Venetian image, still as delicate and transparent as possible, a romantic quality rarely seen in curved steel walkways.

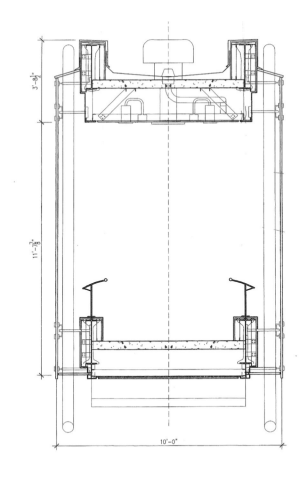

3'-8½"

11'-7⅞"

10'-0"

Inlaid Box *santa clara, california*
GA Lobbies

A similar example of incision in architectural massing and detailing is present in the Inlaid Box lobbies for an office complex next to the Great America Theme Park. These interiors are housed in two diamond-shaped volumes with floor-plates that decrease in size as they rise above the ground and are rotated 45-degrees relative to each other. The corner of each building is slightly chamfered to ease access to the enclosure. Marx chiseled a round, two-story lobby to file off the uninviting edges of its leftover interior. Visitors progress into the round space through a pinch point and pierce into an ante room right before the elevator lobby. The circular elements and the expansion and contraction of these laminated circles dissolve the relentlessness of the exterior architectural form. Vertical stainless steel fins function metaphorically, like the measures of a musical staff defined by the horizontal subdivisions of the cladding panels. In Marx's words, the resulting architectural score is both an etude in steel and wood and also in stone and plaster. This immersive environment constantly keeps the senses on edge. Projections of ceiling patterns on the floor and the insertion of high-end acoustical materials and an intricate metal lay-in soffit culminate in a climax of visual finesse.

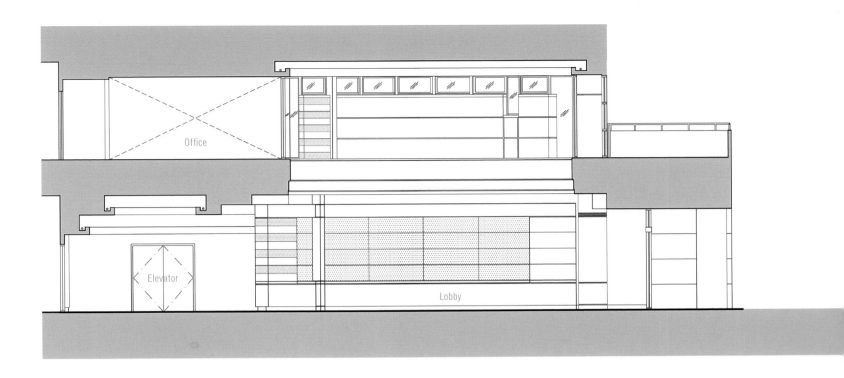

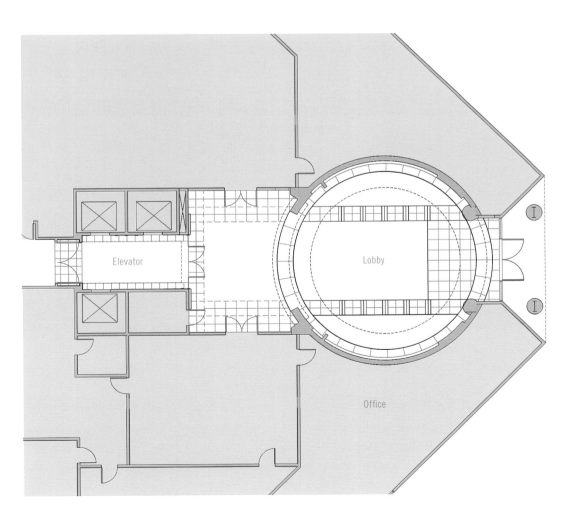

Once this space is discovered hidden behind the anonymity of a given enclosure, what's on display is the intricate meeting of details within details and inlaid designs.

Crashing Waves *tongyeong, korea*
Tongyeong Concert Hall

A change of gear in Marx's design explorations occurred in the recent competition for the design of a concert hall in Tongyeong, South Korea. In this case, what is ordinarily a three-week effort stretched to almost two-months. A trip to the area led to the discovery of a plot of land on an island with commanding views of the downtown district. Exposed on all sides, the site sits sixty feet above the ocean, with two sides defining a cliff and a third side sloping steeply. Marx's team went out on a ferry boat to see the site from the water to absorb an essential viewpoint in the future presence of the complex in the bay. At the onset, this musical compound was to be dedicated to the famous Korean composer Isang Yun (1917-1995), who authored numerous symphonies and chamber works, many of them based on the twelve-tone principle and in later years on the "main-tone" technique. To this date, Yun is a controversial figure, equally a national hero and a villain. During World War II, he opposed the Japanese occupation of Korea and joined the resistance. He moved to Europe in the late 1950s and eventually settled in West Berlin, Germany. In 1963, he took a trip to North Korea that led to a string of unfortunate events in his life. Kidnapped from his home in 1967, he was sentenced to life in prison. Public outcry from governments and musicians, led by Igor Stravinsky, allowed for his release on the condition that he could never go back to his homeland. However, many of his most well-known symphonies were premiered in North Korea even though he was persona non-grata in South Korea. He is now revered, especially in his hometown, and yet still stirs political controversy. Government intervention deflected the intention to honor Yun with this grand complex, and all that remains is a small memorial to his artistic achievements. Marx's project would thus be known as the Tongyong Concert Hall.

A number of schemes were produced, all of them deriving in one way or another from the intensity and vibrancy of Yun's music. Scheme 33, also known as the Crashing Waves, is evocative of the composer's artistic intentions, which makes clashing into an ordering principle, unbridled in its architectonic potential. This option comprises two parts: the upper part, with it metaphorical frozen undulation of water waves, and the podium, which at a ground level starts as a landform that mimics the ocean. This idea followed numerous studies about what kind of elevation and articulation should enclose the tallest pieces in order to reinforce that concept. The calm "water" at the base builds into a spatial crescendo culminating in the vertical glass elements that define the lobby. These elongated pieces become sculptural, slightly arching to become emblematic "foam". Abstracted waves crash together. What follows is an experience modulated in a series of fluid ramps that go from the entry doors down to the parking lot. Fluidity, once again, endows the design with breathtaking dynamism. The reference to the wave informs the massing, the section, and site plan. Symbolically, it is the conflagration of the ocean, the music, and the two Koreas coming together that establishes the conceptual footprint that the plan is built upon, in tribute to the composer's life.

CRASHING WAVES

On some distant
seashore
Isang Yun sits
dreaming

of the day
two powerful
discordant
12-tone waves
will crash

their waters
mixing

aspiring to
a potential future

embracing
a tragic past

-John Marx

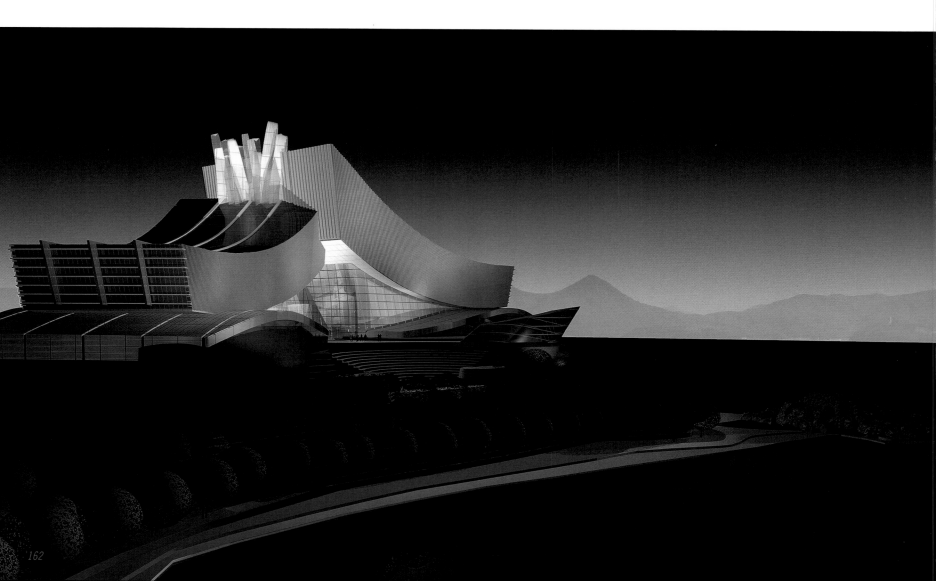

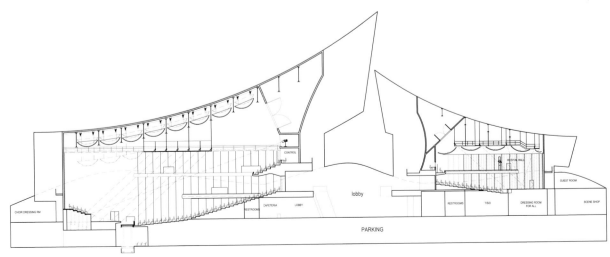

CHOIR DRESSING RM · RESTROOMS · CAFETERIA · LOBBY · CONTROL · lobby · RECITAL HALL · RESTROOMS · T/S/O · DRESSING ROOM FOR ALL · GUEST ROOM · SCENE SHOP

PARKING

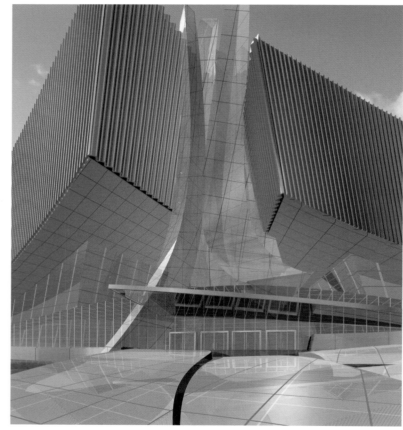

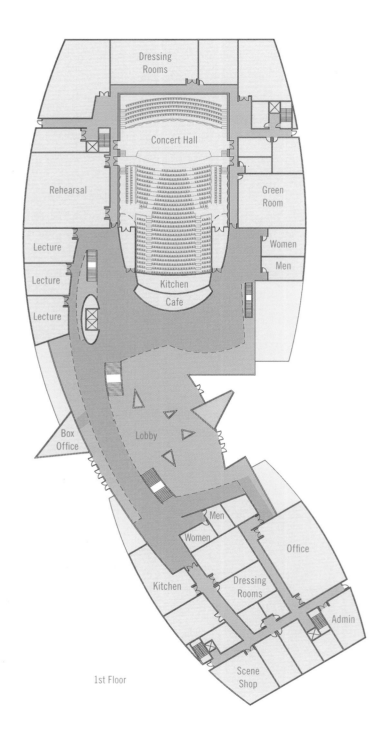

1st Floor

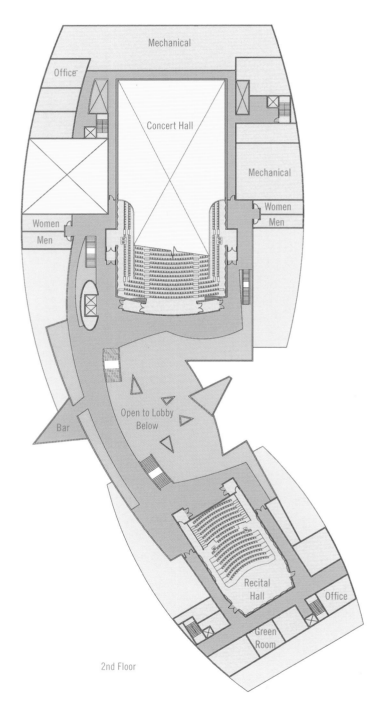

2nd Floor

Wandering the Garden of Technology and Passion

By John Marx

As far back as I can remember I wanted to be an artist. My experience in architecture has shown me that art very often takes a less important role in the design of buildings than I would have ever imagined as a student. This has been a common theme throughout the history of architecture. The Palace of Fine Arts, designed by Bernard Maybeck for the San Francisco 1915 Panama-Pacific Exposition illustrates this in a deliberate manner. High atop the main colonnade are a series of inward looking figures, by sculptor Ulric Henry Ellerhusen, arms embracing large box planters. I remember from college history class these figures were said to be "weeping with the notion of life without art". While I certainly am not advocating a return to Beaux Arts architecture, this sense of architecture as poetry has been lost, to some degree, over the last 50 years.

I do believe architecture is an artform critical to a thriving society which must also balance its pragmatic requirements. Architects, perhaps in a reaction to the romantic excesses of Beaux Arts architecture, have shifted their efforts toward more abstract concepts. Common in most architectural critiques is a deep discussion of "the Big Idea". But rare in these discussions is how the building will relate on an emotional level to the users of the structure. Rare is a discussion of proportion, scale, and texture. Many projects have a clever Big Idea, but are dull and uninspiring. Objective concepts are much easier to discuss than emotions and the subjective grey areas of personal taste. Clients today are uncomfortable with the idea that an architect can create a building of beauty and meaning to the community; they tend to see us as technicians filling a pragmatic need. The lack of subjective discussion fuels this. I would advocate that architects shift toward a greater balance of Concept and Art in their work, and in the educational and critical systems that influence the profession. Powerful and meaningful architecture results when the dynamic balance between Concept and Art flourishes, the absence of either produces a compromised outcome. The delicate balance of these two forces can create a tension that drives the artistic process.

The work presented in this book attempts to show an artistic path, of many possible paths, to add poetry back into architecture. As with most architects I know, I went into architecture with a passion for art as well as the notion of finding a vehicle for contributing to society. How we each charted our path through the profession, and the nature of our contribution, is as different as the uniqueness we possess as human beings. Mine was a bit of a wandering path.

We debated whether *Wandering the Garden of Technology and Passion* was too long, too romantic. We kept it. It seemed to fit the body of work, as well as the underlining connective themes that became apparent to explain the nature of the projects. As outlined below, each part of this title has meaning relative to my artistic development over the past 18 years.

Wandering

In spite of the linear and rational career path I have followed, my actual artistic development has been quite intuitive and non-linear, each inspiration spontaneously following the next.

Garden

There are several themes here. It implies a lush optimism of both mystery and delight. Exotic, sensual, existing in deep shadow and bright sunlight. In this sense, there is the metaphor of the garden, but also a philosophy of art following nature in an organic way.

Technology

Foremost this applies to the advent of the computer in the creative design process and in the process of building projects. This also applies in the role of technology as it affects broad social and cultural change. The computer has prompted deep changes in the world on so many levels it is hard to express the impact.

Passion

This refers to a passion for art as a means of expression, but also, as with technology, how art can affect positive change in society. From this position, expression does not intend to be "self-expression", but the expression of a philosophy of life in balance. Inevitably the tangible form this takes comes from the self, which is what gives it a unique character. In a sense, the building wants to tell you something about life.

Being an Architect

In order to talk about the path I have followed in architecture, it is important to understand the nature of the struggle which architecture presents. "The Struggle" is the adherence to the goal of creating something extraordinary in life, of contributing to society through architecture. This requires intense, unrelenting effort and an enduring commitment. It is inherent in architecture that we always fall short, but the distance we can travel when conditions are right makes the difficulties of the journey worth taking. The great danger within a profession is that it is easy to 'make do', to settle for fulfilling the basic goals of the client, or the public, or the financial requirements of small fees. In this sense, the old artist's maxim "Good is the Enemy of the Great" is very revealing.

Artistic vision is what fuels the passion of an artist. Vision is that ability to imagine something powerful from the context in which we each exist, from within our nature, and which creates something unique. The quality of this vision separates one artist from another. In painting, the artist sees something that moves them and then paints it. For the architect, this is made much more complex by the fact that architecture is commission based.

I tell people what I do as a design partner in an architecture firm is "manage compromise". Once the very brief period passes where you establish "the big idea/formal concept" an overwhelming percentage of your time is dedicated to protecting the design intent from an inevitably slow (or fast) decay leading to a mediocre built form. These negative influences are both internal (inside the firm) as well as external (budgets, clients, contractors, planning departments, etc). An architect's ability to find the best possible outcome from a seemingly impossible set of conditions is key to the success of every project.

Most often people think architecture is fundamentally a pure artistic endeavor, like painting. The reality is that we have a unique, but by nature, limiting relationship with our clients. We serve our clients, and the public, but as artists, we also need to provide vision. A lot of time is well spent communicating this vision to the client. Then there is the business management, technical, and legal side that can consume too much of one's time.

My experience working at both large and small firms is that at best 10% of what architects do tends to be somewhat creative. Of that, for most firms, only 20% is interesting from an artistic standpoint. That means 2% of what you do is what you thought you were going to do after you got out of college. This brings up some very interesting issues with how universities prepare students for professional life. When I was teaching at UC Berkeley, I often asked my students what their impressions were of what life was like after school. Their responses showed that no one really told them what their odds were of being in a design position at any point of time in their careers. Enrollment would certainly shrink if students had a sense of this. Architecture students are some of the most passionate, dedicated, and clever students you will encounter. Many of them leave the profession early out of frustration with the lack of design opportunity.

Practice Models

All of this leads an aspiring architect to wonder what kinds of practice options exist, and this certainly affected my path in the profession. A general view of architecture might lead one to believe there are two kinds of architecture firms, the Service Firm and the Critical Firm.

The Service Firm provides most of what is considered architecture in the US. These firms are built on a business model of budgets and schedules, of quarterly profits made by making sure their design process aligns well with their clients' lower expectations. There are often formulas based on building and client types which serve them well. The goal is to not push their clients out of their comfort zones, or to confront issues that are complex for fear of alienating their clients or creating inefficiencies that would jeopardize their fees. They are quite willing to compromise their training and ideals for this efficiency.

Critical Firms, on the opposite end of the spectrum, generally will not compromise their ideals to suit their client. This is not to say that they do not care deeply about their clients, they do. They believe they provide an art form, which demands the highest levels of "integrity". They will turn away commissions which do not allow the freedom of expression they require to fulfill their goals. Their clients tend to have a high regard for fine art, and the resources to achieve that level of architecture. There is a perception that Critical Firms are arrogant and out of touch with mainstream culture. There is some basis for this criticism of the Critical Firm, but given the "visionary" nature of this practice model, it is not the responsibility, or the focus, of a Critical Firm to worry about this.

From an aspiring architect's standpoint there are more pragmatic issues involved with the Critical Firm practice model, namely, not starving. An old joke in architecture is "To become a great architect, one is born into wealth, married into wealth, or you teach." Another is "How do you create a small fortune in architecture .... start with a large one". While these jokes may seem trite, there is a great deal of truth in them. While a poet or painter can maintain a "day job" in order to pay the bills, and architect is all in, and cannot practice effectively part time.

In the murky grey area between these two exists what I call "Reflective Firms". Reflective firms have high ambitions, are thoughtful about the issues involved with each project. They try to do the best they possibly can, given their limited resources, to create meaningful architecture out of the finite constraints of their projects. They rarely can afford to turn away a project, and, in fact, often relish the challenge of raising the level of art in what might be an otherwise ordinary building. I have wandered into this murky grey area in my path through architecture. Partially this is based on circumstance (I did not fall into one of the three options above) and partially it is philosophical. I believe both Service Firms and Critical Firms provide a value to society, although very different, in each case. Growing up in a rural corner of the Midwest I have always been drawn away from the notion of art as an elite pursuit, and have felt the challenge of operating in this grey area.

Architecture and Music

The dynamic between these three practice models is also based on the quality of our clients, and the social context we currently live in. Most potential clients in the US have very little background or education in architecture and the consumer basis for our current culture focuses on extracting a financial gain from popular media such as music and movies. The closest most Americans will get to architecture is if they remodel or commission a new home.

Designing homes requires a unique and special relationship between client and architect. The home is one's most private place. When a client decides to build a home for themselves they quite justifiably want the home to be a reflection of their individual dreams and aspirations. Hiring an architect to design their home creates an interesting dynamic, which is rarely present for people in the normal course of their lives. The ideal role of the architect is to listen, quite intensely, and to then create an artwork that is an extension of their client's aspirations, which the client could never dream of but, when realized, moves the client emotionally, as any great art should.

Often, clients claim to want architecture as art, but progress as if the architect should only guide them through the process as a trained pencil. They feel they know what they want, it's their house, and the result most often falls unspeakably short of what they could have enjoyed.

The act of purchasing music is sometimes a useful analogy. Most people enjoy music, and a large percentage of them are quite passionate about the music they love. They go to concerts, they buy recorded music. The music they enjoy will invariably fall into genres or styles, that define their tastes. Once they have developed a sense of what they like, they could start writing their own music, learn to play a variety of instruments, and ultimately record their own music. Some people actually do this, and some become quite good at it. The overwhelming percentage of people don't actually get this far, and would rather buy the music of the artists they love. There is a great investment of time and training to become as good as the musicians you love. Why would this be any different with the design of your own home? Why not commission a design which could move you in ways you could not do yourself?

Often times clients balk at an architect's fees or the notion that they need to reduce the size of their home to accommodate these fees. Generally there is a perception of low value seen in the "art" that an architect brings to the construction of a new home. Where did this come from?

Cultural Relevance

Until the advent of Modernism, one of the highest priorities of an architect was to create beauty. In a cultural context this was the bridge that allowed the public to become emo-tionally attached to architecture. People, broadly, respond to beauty. Over the centuries this took many stylistic forms (with differing rules and intentions), but fundamentally, the scale, proportion, and texture of architecture is what speaks to the public.

Modernism changed all that. From my experience in school and in the profession, beauty is not discussed. In many circles it is considered trite and old fashioned, in others it is considered a subjective matter unworthy of adult conversation. The primary focus is on concept or uniqueness. In my view, concept without beauty is not fully architectural. Great works of architecture must resonate on both levels.

The great legacy of Modernism is the notion that architecture, and perhaps more specifically, architects can help instigate positive social change. The ideal of social change is one I grew up with in school in the late 1970s. The idea that architecture was more than an "art form" still resonates throughout the profession.

So, there is this split of Modernism as a style, and Modernism as a social movement. Modernism as a style has settled into a long history of styles in architecture, but it is not a single style. In the early 1980s Postmodernism opened up the rigidity of the "International Style" and with recent innovations in material and computer-aided design and construction, the current trends in modern design have shown an explosion of creativity.

Architecture as a vehicle for social change has disengaged itself from Modernism as a style, as seem most prominently in the "New Urbanist" movement.

The great early modernists had an innate sense of beauty that they brought with them. Modernism is, however, a very difficult style within which to design. A mediocre designer, with training in a historic style, could create a decent building that the general public could appreciate. I believe it takes more talent and skill to design a decent modern building. Hence, in the hands of a great designer, breathtaking modern buildings have been designed. It is in the vast middle ground where architects have failed to reach the public. It is the 90% of what is built in the modern style, especially in the hands of average designers, that feels cold, austere and banal, with no ability to emotionally move the public beyond a feeling of boredom and isolation.

There has also been a shift in US culture toward a "consumer model", where the reward and significance of "art" was based on popular patterns of where people spent their money, rather than a critical system based on a cultured "elite", with a sense of history and "taste". The concept of "fine art" was replaced by, "what sells".

The absence of beauty in mediocre modern architecture, along with a sense of "consumer empowerment" led to the general population rejecting modern architecture as inhumane. The harshest examples of this are communities where design restrictions legislate out the design of modern buildings.

We need to re-engage the public by adding beauty and character back into the design dialogue. Our buildings need to speak once again to the broad human spirit. It may be initially difficult to establish this dialogue, to give beauty a voice that concept primarily now enjoys. Once reconnected, the resulting architecture has a chance to extend the powerful basis of Modern Design, and create a vital new paradigm where the public delights in the experience of new building and we can more fully express the spirit of our times.

FEATURED PROJECTS

2000
nVIDIA HEADQUARTERS
480,000 SF, Santa Clara, CA
Sobrato Development Companies

2001
CARMEL VALLEY CLUB
87,000 SF, San Diego, CA
Western Athletic Clubs

2002
VIOL CENTER
2,000,000 SF, Sao Paulo, Brazil
Collaboration with KMD Architects

INLAID BOX
Great American Corporate Center
1,000 SF, Santa Clara, CA
Sobrato Development Companies

2003
JEJU INTERNATIONAL AIRPORT
500,000 SF Jeju Island, South Korea
Collaboration with Jung IL Architects

HOUSE OF BORROWED LIGHT
2,000 SF, San Francisco, CA

2004
FALLING LOTUS BLOSSUMS
EON Free Zone
4,000,000 SF, Pune, India
Collaboration with NPAPL Architects

2005
BRADBURY MILLS
1,200,000 SF, Mumbai, India
Collaboration with NPAPL Architects

2006
NETFLIX HEADQUARTERS BRIDGE
160,000 SF Los Gatos, CA
Sobrato Development Companies

METROPLEX RETAIL CENTER
500,000 SF, Pune, India
Collaboration with NPAPL Architects

THE ARK
Walnut Creek, CA
The Griggs Group

2007
TECHNOLOGY DRIVE
400,000 SF, San Jose, CA
Sobrato Development Companies

OASIS
500,000 SF, Santa Clara, CA
Sobrato Development Companies

SUBURBAN CANYON
Great American Corporate Center
1,000,000 SF, Santa Clara, CA
Sobrato Development Companies

2008
MONDRIAN'S WINDOW
Beach House
3,500 SF San Francisco, CA

2009
CRASHING WAVES
Tongyeong Concert Hall
500,000 SF, Tongyeong, Korea
Collaboration with
Gansam Architects & J S Fisher

2010
LYRICAL SEASHORE
Kaohsiung Maritime Cultural &
Popular Music Center
1,000,000 SF, Kaohsiung, Tawain
Collaboration with
J S Fisher Architects

BIOGRAPHY
JOHN F. MARX, AIA

EDUCATION
University of Illinois
BSAS 1980, High Honors

AWARDS
AIA SAN MATEO, HONOR AWARD, 2005
House of Borrowed Light

AIA SAN MATEO, HONOR AWARD, 2005
nVidia Headquarters

AIA/JUSTICE NATIONAL DESIGN CITATION, 1998
Klamath County Courthouse

GOLD NUGGET AWARD, 2007
Netflix Headquarters

AIA/SF COMPUTER GRAPHICS EXHIBITS
1st Place, 2D Graphics, Globo, 1999
Hon Mention, WAC- Oasis Persp. 1996
Hon Mention, WAC- Night Scene 1996
Hon Mention, BMW Showroom, 1994

AWARD OF DISTINCTION
BACA 9TH ANNUAL EXHIBITION
Summer 1989 Watercolors

DESIGN COMPETITIONS
First Place Awards
TongYeoung Concert Hall, Korea , 2010
Bradbury Mills, India , 2005
Orange Walk, India, 2005
Asendas, India, 2005
EON Free Zone, India, 2004
MetroPlex Center, India, 2004
Globo HQ, Brazil, 1999
Guaruhlos, Brazil, 1998
MBC Studio, Korea (Tie), 1998
Cha Hospital, Korea, 1996
Panambi, Brazil, 1996

ACADEMIC
LECTURER/INSTRUCTOR
Arch 135: Digital Design
University of California, Berkeley
Spring 1996 to Spring 2000

VISITING LECTURER / CO-INSTRUCTOR
Arch 295x: Architecture and the Internet
University of California, Berkeley
Fall 2001,2002, 2003, 2006, 2007
Spring 2008, Fall 2008

TECHNICAL CO-CHAIR
ACADIA 2003
Indianapolis, Indiana

ALPHA RHO CHI MEDAL
University of Illinois, 1980

EDWARD C EARL PRIZE
First Place Award, Fall 1979

Gargoyle Honor Society
Initiation, Spring 1980

JURY MEMBER AND CRITIC
GUEST DESIGN CRITIC/FINAL JURIES
University of California, Berkeley
Spring 2000, Spring 1996, Fall 1994

GUEST DESIGN CRITIC
University of Illinois, Spring 1999

VIRTUAL JUROR
University of Illinois, Fall 1998

JUROR
Joint Studies Program, 1996-97

REFEREE
"Journal of Construction Research"
Hong Kong, Fall 2000

JUROR
AIA/SF Computer Graphics Exhibit, 1998, 2002

LECTURES
UNIVERSITY OF CALIFORNIA, BERKELEY
'Digital Design-Recent Work'
Summer 1995,96,97,99.00,2001, Spring1996, Fall 00, 03, 2004

UNIVERSITY OF ILLINOIS CHAMPAIGN/URBANA
"Wandering the Garden of Technology and Passion"
March 1999

KYONGGI UNIVERSITY, SEOUL, KOREA
"The Relevance of Digital Design" March 1999

ACADIA, 98 UNIVERSITY OF LAVAL, QUEBEC CITY
"A Proposal for Alternative Methodologies in Teaching Digital Design". Paper Presentation, October 1998

ACADIA, 98 UNIVERSITY OF LAVAL, QUEBEC CITY
Conference Panel Member
"Education vs. Technology: Taming the Beast vs. Goring Sacred Cows" October 1998

UNIVERSITY OF SYDNEY, AUSTRALIA
"The Relevance of Digital Design" July 1998

TECHNION UNIVERSITY, HAIFA, ISRAEL
"Direct Digital Design " March 1998

PUBLICATIONS
CITY BY DESIGN – SAN FRANCISCO
Panache Partners, Inc., 2009

1000 X ARCHITECTURE OF THE AMERICAS
Verlaghuas-Braun, Berlin, 2009

DREAM HOMES OF SAN FRANCISCO
Panache Partners, Inc., 2007

ROBB REPORT VACATION HOMES
"Fog City Redux"
Jorge Arango, February, 2007, p. 84 – 95.

ARCHITECTURE'S NEW MEDIA Yehuda Kalay
MIT Press, Cambridge Mass. 2004
(Cover Design, Co-Author Chapter 24)

HISTORY OF FORM•Z Pierluigi Serraino.
Princeton Architectural Press, 2002
(Design Projects, Digital Design Technique)

ARTIST'S IMPRESSIONS IN ARCHITECTURAL DESIGN
Gidding, Horne. Spon Press, London, Great Britain, 2002. (San Tomas, Oral-B, Digital Design Technique), pp. 138,142,166.

ACADIA, 2001, (ed. Jabi and Majkowski),
"Architecture and the Internet: Designing Places in

Cyberspace". Yehuda Kalay and John Marx, Buffalo, NY 2001

VSMM"01, (Addison, ed.)
"The Role of Place in Cyberspace" Yehuda Kalay and John Marx, Berkeley, CA 2001

ARCHITECTURAL RECORD (Form4 Firm Profile)
"Giving Small Firms the Tools to be Big"
B.J.Novitski, Feb 2000, p.141-142.

ARCHITECTURE WEEK Inaugural Issue
(Form4 Firm Profile)" Small Firm makes it Big"
B.J.Novitski, May2000,
www.ArchitectureWeek.com/2000/0517/tools_1-1.
html

ARCHITECTURE WEEK
" Course Goes Digital" John Marx, August 2000
http://www.ArchitectureWeek.com/2000/0823/
tools_1-1.html

CYBERSPACE: THE WORLD OF ETHEREAL ARCHITECTURE
Images Press, Sydney, Australia, 2000.
(Study for a 120 Story Tower), pp. 186-187.

CADALYST Design Spotlight B.J.Novitski, October 2000, (Design Process Profile)

AUTOMATION IN CONSTRUCTION 9
"A Proposal for Alternative Methodologies in Teaching Digital Design". John Marx, Spring 2000

ARCHITECTURAL RECORD (Globo)
"San Francisco Firm Contributes to an Ever-Expanding Sao Paulo" Ellen Sands, May 1999, p.100.

URBAN LAND INSTITUTE (Globo)
"Brazil's Tower of the Future" March 1999

ARCHITECTURAL RECORD (Klamath County Courthouse) "Courthouses: Designing Justice for All". Todd S. Phillips, AIA, March 1999, p.107.

ARCHITECTURAL RECORD (Remarks)
"Digital Architect"
B.J.Novitski, April 1999, p.39-40.

ARQUITECTURA DIGITAL (KIDC)
"Metodologia de Diseno Digital"
John Marx, January 1999

ACADIA, 98 COMPUTERS IN THE DESIGN STUDIO, ed. Seebohm and Van Vyck, "A Proposal for Alternative Methodologies in Teaching Digital Design". John Marx, October 1998

SPACE MAGAZINE, ISSUE no. 369
Korean International Design Center
June 1998 (Project Feature)

KAPLAN McLAUGHLIN DIAZ.
PLACEMAKING: INNOVATION AND INDIVIDUALITY,
Richard Rapaport 1998, Rockport Publishers, Inc., Gloucester, MA. p.10, 188-189.

AEMJ JOURNAL
"Digital Design: A Revolutionary Tool"
August 1996 (Profile)

COMPUTER GRAPHICS WORLD
"Creating 3D Spaces With 3d Tools"
November 1995 (User Profile)

ARCHITECTURAL RECORD
"The Computer as a Presentation Tool"
June 1994
SF EXAMINER

"Art in CADD" / BMW Showroom
13 July 1994

ARTS & ARCHITECTURE
"Analysis of Historicism in Architecture "
Fall 1982 Co-Author

NATIONAL SCIENCE FOUNDATION
"Development of Daycare for the Aged"
Summer 1979 Co-Author

EXHIBITIONS
Architecture
YALE UNIVERSITY
Department of Architecture
"Digital Media Exhibition" (UCB Students)
New Haven, CT, 2000

CATHOLIC UNIVERSITY
"Arch 135, The Work of Students from UC Berkeley"
Washington, DC, 2000

TECHNICAL UNIVERSITY, BERLIN
"Digital Exploration, Content to From 1996 to 2000"
Berlin, Germany, 2001

AIA/NY MODERN COURTHOUSE EXHIBIT
New York, NY, 1997

AIA COMPUTER GRAPHICS EXHIBIT
San Francisco, CA
1993,1994,1995,1996,1998,1999

ANSEL ADAMS CENTER
"Evolution of Digital Art "
San Francisco, CA, Sept. 1994

ARCHITECTURAL RECORD
"The Computer as a Presentation Tool"
Touring: NY, NY. /Washington DC, 1994

EXHIBITIONS
Watercolors
JIM LOUGHLIN
Private Collection
San Francisco, CA, 2009

FOX/LAGRECA GALLERY
San Francisco, CA, 1994

ERIKSSON AND ELINS
San Francisco, CA, 1990-92

GUMP'S
San Francisco, CA, 1989

MANCHESTER GALLERY
Pittsburgh, PA, 1990

MANOA GALLERY
Honolulu, HI, 1989

SAN BERNARDINO CO. MUSEUM
San Bernardino, CA, 1989

BACA 9th ANNUAL EXHIBIT
Berkeley, CA, 1989

CLOROX CORP.
Permanent Collection
Oakland, CA 1991

KAISER PERMANENTE
Permanent Collection
Oakland, CA, 1991

PROJECT LIST

CORPORATE

LAWSON LANE
500,000 sf, Santa Clara, CA

TECHNOLOGY DRIVE
400,000 sf, San Jose, CA

NETFLIX HEADQUARTERS
160,000 sf, Los Gatos, CA

STATE INSURANCE COMP FUND
120,000 sf, Redding, CA

ASCENDAS Campus
2,000,000 sf, Kolkata, India

COMMERCE ONE
780,000 sf, Dublin, CA

PUNE SOFTWARE PARK
4,000,000 sf, Pune, India

GREAT AMERICAN CORP CENTER
1,000,000 sf, Santa Clara, CA

COYOTE VALLEY
566,000 sf, San Jose, CA

nVIDIA HEADQUARTERS
480,000 sf, Santa Clara, CA
AIA Honor Award

CYBERPORT TOWER
250,000 sf, Hong Kong, China

ADOBE SYSTEMS HQ
450,000 sf, East Palo Alto, CA

LAM RESEARCH INC.
120,000 sf, Fremont, CA

FARIA LIMA FINANCIAL CENTER
450,000 sf, Sao Paulo, Brazil

SAO LUIS
540,000 sf, Sao Paulo, Brazil

UN INT'L. VACCINE INSTITUTE
340,000 sf, Seoul, Korea

MERCK LABORATORIES
395,000 sf, Mexico City, Mexico

MERCK HEADQUARTERS
75,000 sf, Santa Fe, Mexico City

ORAL-B CORP. HEADQUARTERS
120,000 sf, Belmont, CA

BOEHRINGER MANNHEIM-ROCHE
550,000 sf, Pleasanton, CA

CIVIC | INSTITUTIONAL

KAOHSIUNG MARITIME CULTURAL &
POPULAR MUSIC CENTER
1,000,000 sf, Kaohsiung, Tawain

TONGYEONG CONCERT HALL
500,000 sf, Tongyeong, Korea

JEJU INTERNATIONAL AIRPORT
500,000 sf, Jeju Island, South Korea

DOMINICAN SCHOOL OF PHILOSOPHY
AND THEOLOGY
15,000 sf, Berkeley, CA

ST. PETERS CHURCH
30,000 sf, LeMoore, CA

GUANGZHOU GRAND OPERA
483,000 sf, Guangzhou, China

KOREAN INTERNATIONAL DESIGN
CENTER
780,000 sf, Bundang, Korea

KLAMATH FALLS COURTHOUSE
80,000 sf, Klamath Falls, Oregon

KLAMATH FALLS COUNTY ADMIN
60,000 sf, Klamath Falls, OR

BISHOP RANCH FINE ARTS MUSEUM
21,000 sf, San Ramon, CA

STEAMFITTERS UNION HQ
48,000 sf, Concord, CA

MBC STUDIOS
940,000 sf, Seoul, Korea

PEOPLE'S HOSPITAL #1
540,000 sf, Shanghai, China

CHA HOSPITAL EXTENSION
120,000 sf, Seoul, Korea

URBAN MIXED USE | RETAIL | HOSPITALITY

GROWEL PLAZA
650,000 sf, Mumbai, India

PALM SPRINGS WEST
2,100,000 sf, Beijing, China

BRADBURY MILLS
1,200,000 sf, Mumbai, India

ORANGE WALK
1,000,000 sf Nagpur, India

METROPLEX RETAIL CENTER
500,000 sf, Pune, India

VIOL CENTER
2,000,000 sf, Sao Paulo, Brazil

GLOBO HEADQUARTERS II
300,000 sf, Sao Paulo, Brazil

SETIN CENTER
300,000 sf, Campinas, Brazil

GLOBO HEADQUARTERS
300,000 sf, Sao Paulo, Brazil

DAEWOO TOWER
3,500,000 sf, Inchon, Korea

XIAMEN CENTER
2,000,000 sf, Xiamen, China

GUARUHLOS CENTER
365,000 sf Sao Paulo, Brazil

INDRA TOWER
950,000 sf, Surabaya, Indonesia

UNIVERSITY CENTER
550,000 sf, East Palo Alto, CA

TOMLINSON CENTER
1,540,000 sf, Singapore

TURTLE CREEK - RITZ CARLTON
1,000,000 sf, Dallas, TX

FISHERMAN'S WHARF HOTEL
100,000 sf, San Francisco, CA

DAIEI RETAIL CENTER
1,500,000 sf, Fukuoka, Japan

MASTER PLANNING

SONG DO TOWN
17,000,000 sf, Inchon, Korea

PUNE SOFTWARE PARK
4,000,000 sf, Pune, India

DINE/ HINES DEVELOPMENT
3,000,000 sf, Santa Fe, Mexico

TAINAN MIXED USE
5,000,000 sf, Tainan, Taiwan

PANAMBI MIXED USE
2,000,000 sf, Sao Paulo, Brazil

CHUN SHEN CITY
53,000 People, Shanghai, China

TAMBORE RETAIL CENTER
800,000 sf, Sao Paulo, Brazil

TECHNION UNIVERSITY
300 Acres, Haifa, Israel

PACIFIC SHORES
1,500,000 sf, Redwood City, CA

HEWLETT PACKARD
600,000 sf, San Jose, CA

MAWUN BAY RESORT
1,100,000 sf, Lombok, Indonesia

ATHLETIC CLUBS | RESORTS

UCSF FITNESS CENTER
10,000 sf, San Francisco

THE SAN FRANCISCO BAY CLUB
45,000 sf, San Francisco, CA

THE ALAMEDA CLUB
55,000 sf, Alameda, CA

CARMEL VALLEY CLUB
87,000 sf, San Diego, CA

ELKS LODGE
80,000 sf, Palo Alto, CA

WESTERN ATHLETIC CLUB
120,000 sf, Walnut Creek, CA

SAUSALITO ATHLETIC RESORT
100,000 sf Club, Sausalito, CA

PACIFIC ATHLETIC CLUB
105,000 sf, Tigard, OR

SAN DIEGO TENNIS CLUB
57,000 sf, San Diego, CA

MARIN BAY CLUB
87,000 sf, Corte Madera, CA

CALIFORNIA TENNIS CLUB
20,000 sf, San Francisco, CA

RESIDENTIAL
Multi Unit | Residential

PALM SPRINGS WEST
600 Units, 2,100,000 sf
Beijing, China

THE ARK
11 Units, Walnut Creek, CA

PUNE GARDENS
500 Units, Pune, India

LOS GATOS GATEWAY
300 Units, 120,000 sf Office
Los Gatos, CA

MASSACHUSETTS CENTER
160,000 sf, Washington, DC

NOVA D'JUHLO
240,000 sf, Sao Paulo, Brazil

UNIVERSITY CENTER HOUSING
40,000 sf, East Palo Alto, CA

TOMLINSON CENTER
1,540,000 sf, Singapore

TURTLE CREEK
1,000,000 sf, Dallas, TX

RUA MARANHAO
220,000 sf, Sao Paulo, Brazil

RESIDENTIAL
Private | Residential

MONDRIAN'S WINDOW
Beach House
3,500 sf, San Francisco, CA

HOUSE OF BORROWED LIGHT
2,000 sf, San Francisco, CA
AIA Honor Award

CARREKER APARTMENT
2,000 sf, San Francisco, CA

OSPREY HOUSE
5,000 sf, Brookings, OR

CHATEAUX DUVALLON
18,000 sf, Napa, CA

DAVID PACKARD JR. HOME
6,000 sf, Los Altos Hills, CA

BIBLIOGRAPHY

Chávez, Carlos. *Musical Thought. Vols. Charles Eliot Norton lectures, 1958-1959.* Cambridge, MA: Harvard University Press, 1961.

Eliot, T S. *Four Quartets.* New York, NY: Harcourt, Brace and Co., 1943.

Goldberger, Paul. *Why Architecture Matters.* New Haven, CT: Yale University Press, 2009.

Harvey, David. *The Condition of Postmodernity.* Cambridge, MA: Blackwell, 1989.

Peter, John. *The Oral History of Modern Architecture: Interviews with the Greatest Architects of the Twentieth Century.* New York, NY: Abrams, 1994.

Smith, Dana K. *Building Information Modeling: a strategic implementation guide for architects, engineers,constructors, and real estate asset managers.* Hoboken, NJ: Wiley, 2009.

WATERCOLOR TITLES

p.6	American Nostalgia, 10" x 16", 1989
p.12	Confluence of Still Waters, 9 " x 12", 1987
p.14t	UKI-E: Woman at Leisure, 9 " x 9", 1988
p.14m	Composition in Muted Primaries, No.2, 6 " x 6", 1988
p.14b	Sinew, 4 " x 8", 1985
p.15.1	Anonymous Passage, 15 " x 15", 1989
p.15.2	Shadow of a Hanging Lamp, 10 " x 10", 1991
p.15.3	UKI-E: First Snowfall, 6 " x 6", 1982
p.15.4	Cartesian Imposition No.2, 6 " x 17", 1987
p.15.5	Unadorned Juxtaposition of Urban Forms, 10" x 10", 1990
p.15.6	Caprice of Nature, 6 " x 6", 1983
p.15.7	Composition in Yellow and Blue No.3, 6 " x 6", 1990
p.15.8	Enigma in Green and Blue, No.3, 6 " x 6", 1986
p.15.9	Abstraction from Nature, No.3, 10 " x 10", 1990
p.168	Abstraction in Black and Pale Yellow, No.8, 10 " x 10", 1989
p.172	Idyllic and Distant Sea, 9 " x 9", 1990
p.168	Momentary Serenity, 9 " x 9", 1988
p.177	Abstraction from Nature No. 2, 10" x 10", 1989

Appendix

Place Matrix

At its most fundamental level, Place exists when an individual (or group) imbues a space with meaning on a personal (emotional) level. On a higher level, there are active and passive senses of place. An active place combines an activity (or activities) with a meaningful space. A passive place does not require direct activity or interaction to be meaningful, its mere existence is sufficient.

There are many types and scales of place. This tends to create a great deal of confusion when trying to describe what "Place" means, as the root meanings will change depending on the type and scale of place. Places are important because when an individual (or group) imbues a space with meaning on a personal level "good things" tend to happen. What these "good things" are varies with the type and scale of the place.

A good thing for a plaza might be its active use by the neighborhood and community due to the quality of its spatial character and the food at the various cafes and restaurants that line its edges. This might create a greater social bond between the people who use this plaza, and therefore the community takes care of each other to a higher degree. A good thing for a downtown museum might be that it defines the spirit of the city or the era and attracts tourists who come to visit.

Architecture has had an uneven relationship with the concept of place-making, of what even constitutes place. There is a tendency for different groups of designers to focus on one type of place, to the partial exclusion of the others. The fine arts based designers will tend to discuss their projects from a metaphoric and symbolic viewpoint. The more pragmatic designers will focus on program, user/neighborhood interests.   An even smaller subset of this group looks at the environmental psychology aspects of place. The design work presented here attempts to combine these two extremes with projects that are both iconic and useable places, and which will have meaning for a broad range of users and the general public.

The following Place Matrices graphically show the types, activators, and target users for 15 of the projects in this monograph.

Place as Icon, Place as "people space" is the combined intention for this project based in Pune India. The difficulty was in finding a form that could be both metaphorically related to the local culture, related in image to high technology, and provide a strong and powerful object in the landscape, that would create a destination in the region. The "Lotus Blossom" conceptually fit these requirements, as an abstracted form it also afforded several opportunities for "people spaces".

Falling Lotus Blossoms - EON SEZ

		Place Type	Description	Activators	Target Users
Formal Rational	Lotus Blossom Form is a metaphor for Indian history and natural plant forms				
		1 Iconic -Metaphor	Lotus Blossom Form is a metaphor for Indian history and natural plant forms	Presence of form in the landscape	Long and medium distance views by pedestrians, and car passengers
		2 Atrium Space	7 story interior social atrium space, axial to building entry.	Café, garden, tables, seating	Office workers
Context	Context - Strong and unique form rises from a sloping hillside. Remote from adjacent development	**3** Courtyard	Exterior Garden Space is a small oasis in the center of each office pod	Sculptural sunshades, seating, landscape, colored lighting	Office workers
		4 Park	Large garden space, central to office park	Landscape, pathways, seating areas	General public, Office workers

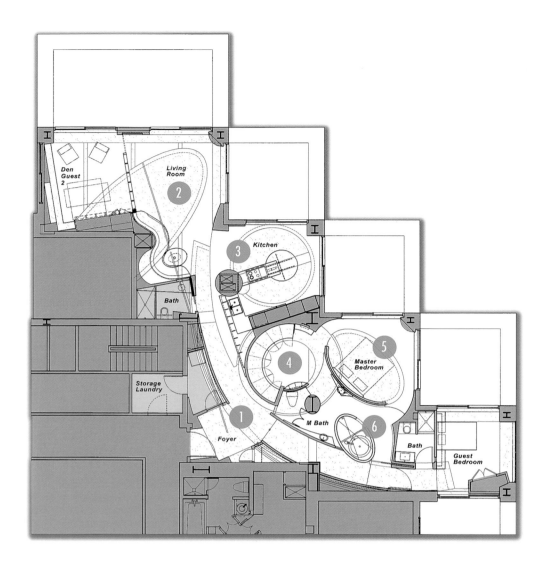

The first visit to the client's penthouse was one of those classic, deeply chilling and foggy San Francisco evenings. Walking out onto the 43rd floor balcony we felt the full immensity of this rolling, swirling drama, the lights of distant buildings coming in and out of view. The client's primary objective was to create a unique place, minimal and imaginative. This evening stayed with me during the design process and provided the undercurrent for the concept.

House of Borrowed Light		Place Type	Description	Activators	Target Users
	1	Symbolic Entry Space	Entry Space incorporates mural of client's cultural heritage and family history	Entry at major circulation hub, Mural.	Private Residence
Formal Rational	San Francisco's natural environs of wind, mist, and fog	2	Defined Spatiality	Living room focuses on fireplace and view over decks. Northern end of penthouse experience. Primary entertainment space.	Bay views, SF Landmark views, fireplace	Private Residence
Context	Interior space is in contrast to context of orthogonal building forms	3	Defined Spatiality	Minimalist kitchen space cantered around a circular glass breakfast table	Kitchen counter social space	Private Residence
		4	Defined Spatiality	Arcing closets surround central dressing area	Dressing Area	Private Residence
		5	Defined Spatiality	Arcing Glass headwall embraces master bed, flows into adjacent spaces	Master bedroom	Private Residence
		6	Formal Landmark	Oval etched glass shower creates a landmark formal ending to the fluid corridor	Provides light at end of corridor.	Private Residence

		Place Type	Description	Activators	Target Users
The Ark	1	Iconic Form	The splayed "C" shaped form create a strong Iconic Landmark Gateway to a new TOD neighborhood		Rapid Transit passengers arriving in Walnut creek and building tenants
Formal Rational — The splayed "C" shaped form create an Iconic Landmark for the TOD neighborhood	2	Aspirational	Street facing double height penthouse space creates aspirational draw to transit users, and pedestrians	Main Living space	
Context — 4-story massing is set by Walnut Creek's density goals	3	Aspirational	Three sets of forms delineate each double height penthouse unit	Balconies and views	

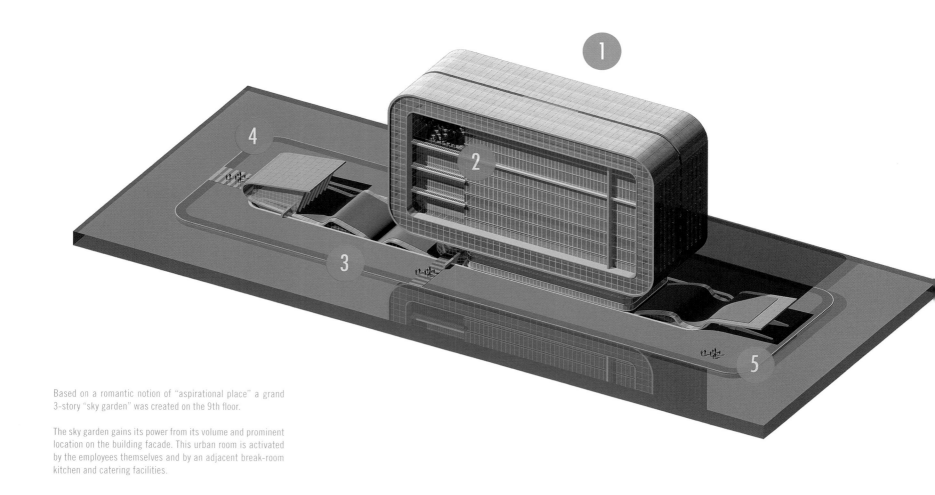

Based on a romantic notion of "aspirational place" a grand 3-story "sky garden" was created on the 9th floor.

The sky garden gains its power from its volume and prominent location on the building facade. This urban room is activated by the employees themselves and by an adjacent break-room kitchen and catering facilities.

			Place Type	Description	Activators	Target Users
Oasis		1	Iconic- Metaphoric Form	Major form is a metaphor for innovation and high tech products created in Silicon Valley.		Long and medium distance views by pedestrians, car passengers
Formal Rational	Major form is a metaphor for innovation and high tech products created in Silicon Valley.	2	Aspirational Place	3 story void punched thru building mass creates an aspirational employee recreation and lunch space	Sky garden, café, seating, landscape, distant views	Office workers
Context	2-story base and café form relate to pedestrian scale. Building massing reflects higher density of transit developments	3	Art Park	Undulating landforms creates areas for sitting, lunching and sculpture. Form becomes the floor and roof of the Café.	Lawn for seating, adjacent café, lobby	General public, office workers
		4	Activated Form	Public Café is created by an extension of undulating landscape forms.	Café, dining, office meetings	General public, office workers
		5	Park	Undulating landforms creates areas for sitting and sculpture. Form becomes the roof of the garage entry	Lawn for seating, adjacent to pedestrian office areas at building base	General public, office workers

There is a music to the ocean, to the rhythm and power of the waves, and in the dynamic elegance of the creatures of the sea. Oceangoing ships and boats, made by man, also follow this musical sense of formal potency.

The intention is to combine these forms of the ocean with the client's popular music program and create a new city scale urban destination. The location and spacing of major program elements allowed the creation of a dynamic and lively civic core that is activated night and day. Here the inflexible grid of Kaohsiung opens up to embrace the fluidity and poetry of the sea.

Lyrical Seashore

Formal Rational — The fluid dynamics of music, water, and sea life form the metaphoric basis of this design.

Context — A variety of building scales relates to general district scale. Curving forms are unique to project.

	Place Type	Description	Activators	Target Users
1	Iconic Landmark	600-ft-tall observation tower in a variation of a sail form serves as a major urban landmark for this dense downtown district.	Observation space, retail-gift shop at tower base	General public, tourists Long and medium distance views by general public
2	Aspirational Endpoint	Viewpoint at end of arcing major pedestrian pathway.	Ocean viewpoint, seating	General public
3	Plaza	Waterfront plaza in the foreground of the Maritime Cultural Museum. Space focuses on art park and views of the water.	Covered café, retail, adjacent to major ferry terminal, observation tower	General public, museum goers.
4	Transit Point	Inner Harbor Ferry Terminal is a major mass transit portal to the surrounding urban area. Glass structure is in the form of a ship's prow.	Ferry terminal, ticketing, small café.	Ferry riders, tourists
5	Cultural Icon	5,500-seat major performance space created within an fluid iconic form	Cultural events, music hall of fame, café, retail.	General public, concert goers
6	Plaza	Large urban event plaza with direct access to the water and connections to the two major performance anchors	Water, cafes, retail, seating, landscape. Adjacent to major cultural event spaces	General public, event goers
7	Grove	Quiet waterfront grove of trees	Water, cafes, retail, seating, landscape. Adjacent to major cultural event spaces	General public
8	Activated Pathway	This waterfront strip will be the nighttime and weekend urban hotspot for popular culture. Also provides daytime food and retail, some of the outdoor café spaces are covered	150-400 seat performance venues, retail, bars, restaurants	General public, concert goers
9	Event Space	12,000-seat outdoor performance space with water views. This venue creates a massive amount of pedestrian traffic into the site.	Outdoor performance space	General public, concert goers
10	Portal Landmark	5-story framed project portal creates an epic scale for the primary entry from the major urban axis addressing the site	Major auto and pedestrian entry point. Massive pedestrian flows. Water to city view connection.	General public

The idea of a second-floor bridge connecting the four buildings that makeup the nVidia Campus initially came from a client request. We saw an opportunity to create an expressive form, which could both unite the campus, but at the same time make a poetic statement which would signify the "heart" of the project. We added two balconies to the otherwise constant 8-foot section of the walkway. We imagined these balconies could become casual meeting areas during the nine months of pleasant weather Silicon Valley enjoys.

A few years later the client reported that "The Squiggle" had not only become a popular meeting spot with general employees, but that the CEO regularly had small meetings out there. They ended up adding several benches to create a lively "street". What had started as an expensive convenience, turned out to be "one of the best investments we ever made". The 8-foot width was key in providing enough space for small groups to meet, but also allowing people to pass by without feeling they were intruding.

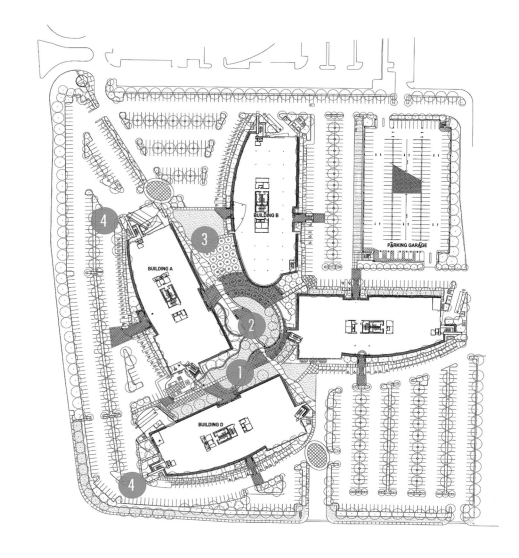

		Place Type	Description	Activators	Target Users
Serpentine - nVidia HQ					
	1	Bridge	Second floor bridge, in the shape of a broad squiggle, links the four building campus together. The squiggle also defines the major landscape element	Major circulation path, small meeting landmark.	Office workers
Formal Rational	The granite prow, the squiggle, village of forms				
	2	Park	Central commons is the heart of the campus, defined by the serpentine bridge	Campus cafeteria, outdoor stage, seating, landscape, water element.	Office workers
Context	Context - 3-story buildings relates to district development and pedestrian scale.				
	3	Grove	Quiet grove provides an alternative to the busier Central Commons	Shaded park, seating	Office workers
	4	Iconic Element	A 3-story green granite wedge serves as an iconic marker and references a ships prow to create a dramatic identity for the campus.		Medium distance views by pedestrians, car passengers

On my first visit to Brazil, our client greeted us with a small cup of incredibly intense coffee, which was both a source of pride and a common business ritual. This unique Brazilian "culture of coffee" unfolded at great depth though out our trip. It came as no surprise later when the concept of a neighborhood plaza based on adding cafes went over well with VIOL.

Café Culture - VIOL HQ

Formal Rational	Double towers capped with sky gardens create a landmark in this section of Sao Paulo
Context	Context - 3-story base relates to district development and pedestrian scale.. Towers relate to downtown Sao Paulo scale.

	Place Type	Description	Activators	Target Users
1	Aspirational Icon	Double towers placed symmetrically create vertical drama at an important urban corner. Each tower is capped with an 11,000 sf sky garden, with an iconic roof form.	Sky garden, café, seating, landscape, distant views	Office workers, general public (with reservations) Long and medium distance views by pedestrians, car passengers.
2	Plaza	Corner landscape plaza creates an inviting pedestrian entry portal to the project.	Corner park, seating, landscape, major entry point to office towers and retail mall	General public, office workers
3	Atrium - Galleria	Interior retail mall provides an urban refuge from the hot Brazilian climate	Interior retail mall	General public, office workers
4	Activated Pathway	Thru block connection is lined with retail on both sides to create an active neighborhood scale	Retail, cafes, restaurants, seating, landscape	General public, office workers
5	Formal Plaza	Large urban plaza with generous open space creates a foreground to the project, and add relief to the density of the neighborhood.	Landscape islands, seating areas, water features, adjacent to major retail area.	General public, office workers
6	Neighborhood Plaza	A generously landscaped oval sculpture garden forms the center of an intimate plaza.	Cafes, retail, restaurants, landscape, seating, art park, adjacent to theater.	General public, office workers, concert goers.
7	Cultural Icon	The curvaceous iconic forms of this legitimate theater provide a cultural activity anchor to this urban neighborhood and plaza	Lobby fronts on a generous plaza, surrounded by cafes, retail, restaurants,	General public, concert goers

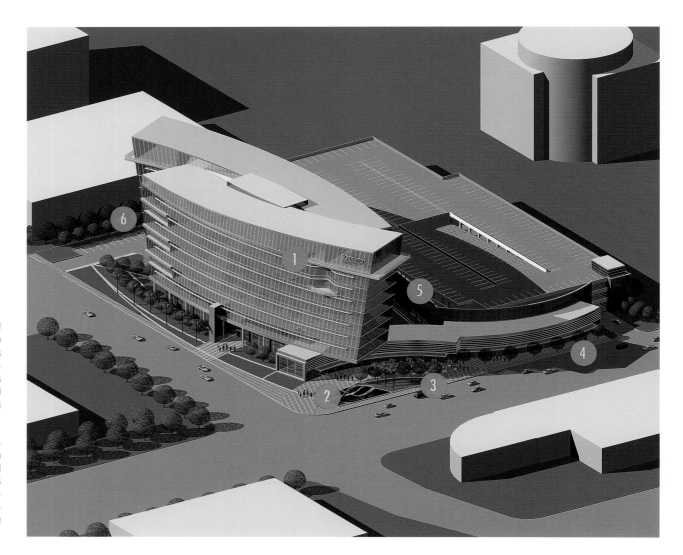

Walkability is a fundamentally missing aspect of life in San Jose, and Silicon Valley in general. New City of San Jose planning department guidelines encourage the creation of pedestrian oriented experiences with in this vacuum. This project uses two broad curves to create a corner art plaza and a retail presence, activating an otherwise bleak urban landscape.

Unfortunately this same planning institution discourages sensual expressive architecture in search of a rigid grid. Where a curve can create a fluid dynamic space for lively urban interaction, on this corner, a straight line would have left a great potential unfulfilled. This project challenges this notion and tries to show that the curve can humanize the urban landscape without overpowering it.

		Place Type	Description	Activators	Target Users
Reflective Aspiration - Technology Drive	1	Aspirational Icon	Curved balcony and 2 story void (invert of balcony plan) cut into arcing building form creates a powerful icon.	Distant views, large enough for gatherings.	Office workers. Long and Medium distance views by pedestrians, car passengers
Formal Rational	An iconic balcony inset into a broad arc creates powerful drama for this corner office tower	2	Plaza	This corner plaza creates a generous pedestrian place, carved out of the urban fabric, by a 2-story arc, but dramatized by the cantilevered arc of the office tower above.	Café, seating, retail, landscape	General public, office workers.
Context	Context - 2-story base relates to district development and pedestrian scale. Towers relate to downtown San Jose scale.	3	Art Park	Thin elegant landscape oasis serves as a background for a major public art installation.	Café, seating, retail, landscape	General public, office workers.
		4	Activated Pathway	Retail frontage activates streetscape and hides garage from pedestrian view.	Retail, café, generous sidewalk, street trees	General public, office workers.
		5	Park	Office worker linear pocket park.	Lobby, garage to office cross pathway, seating, landscape, water feature, art.	Office workers
		6	Aspirational Detail	Small balconies provide aspirational outdoor spaces.	Distant Views. Office and conference room access	Office workers

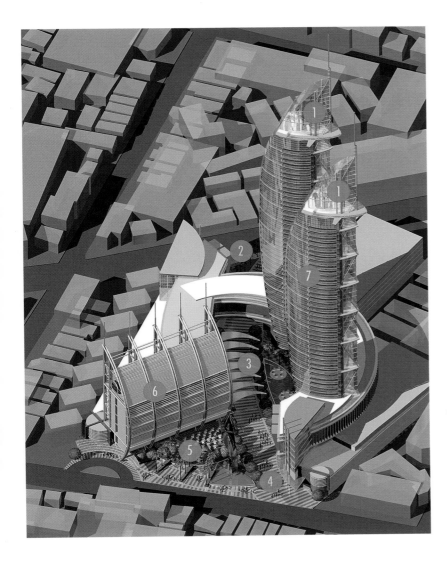

The iconic and highly aspirational places in this project are the sky gardens at the tops of each tower, but the real community place is on the ground level. Carved out of the center of the development is a huge open space, which serves as a neighborhood oasis. This place is part plaza, part event space, part water garden with dining islands. It is sheltered from the chaos of urban Mumbai, yet because it sits aside a through-block pedestrian way it affords quiet people watching opportunities.

Sanctuary - Bradbary

		Place Type	Description	Activators	Target Users
	1	Aspirational Icon	Sky gardens at tower tops provide both an aspirational icon signature, as well as garden space for the tenants.	Sky garden, catering kitchen, seating, tables, landscape, distant views	Condo residents, outside event rentals
Formal Rational — A series of sail forms, in the two condo towers and the hotel	**2**	Plaza - Activated Pathway	This entry plaza, off the smaller street, invites you into The Grand Arc, an activated pathway, that connects to the larger street.	Retail, cafes, restaurants, seating, landscape	General public, office workers, hotel guests, shoppers, condo residents
Context — Context - 3-story base relates to district development and pedestrian scale. Towers relate to downtown Mumbai scale.	**3**	Neighborhood Plaza	Large central plaza, protected from harsh sun, creates an oasis of retail shops and cafes .	Café-Restaurant, seating areas, landscape, retail shops, water features, seating islands.	General public, office workers, hotel guests, shoppers, condo residents
	4	Plaza - Activated Pathway	This entry plaza, off the larger street, invites you into the Grand Arc, an activated pathway, that connects to the smaller street.	Retail, cafes, restaurants, seating, landscape	General public, office workers, hotel guests, shoppers, condo residents
	5	Formal Plaza	Large urban plaza with generous open space creates a foreground to the project, and add relief to the density of the neighborhood.	Landscape islands, seating areas, water features, adjacent to major retail area.	General public, office workers, hotel guests, shoppers, condo residents
	6	Iconic Form	Hotel's bold shape echoes towers		Medium distance views by pedestrians, car passengers

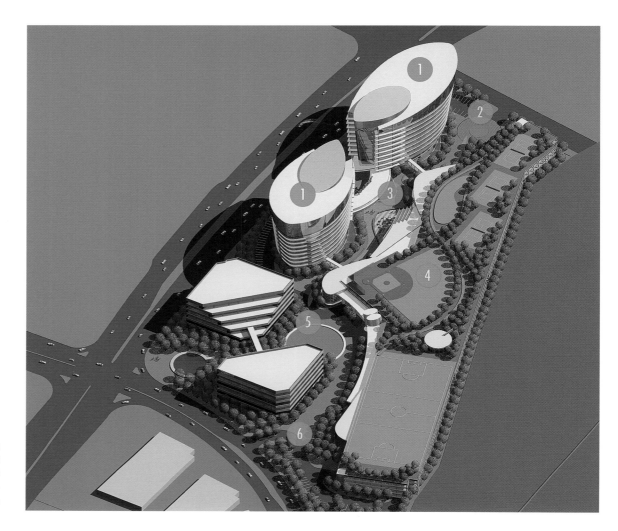

The fair weather of Silicon Valley affords the chance for this man-made suburban canyon to enliven the experience of working in Santa Clara. It is in a sense a landscaped street activated by the communal activities that bring people together; cafes, meeting rooms, fitness center, etc. Like a canyon its lushness and intimacy are intended to draw you in, entice you to sit down with your laptop and start working.

Suburban Canyon - GA Campus

		Place Type	Description	Activators	Target Users
	1	Iconic Form	The two tower forms are a metaphor for innovation and high technology created in Silicon Valley.		Long and Medium distance views by pedestrians, car passengers
Major Formal Rational — Iconic Tower Forms, suburban activated canyon space	2	Entry Plaza	Entry plaza invites you into The Canyon, an activated pathway, that connects thru the entire project.	Major auto and pedestrian entry point.	General Public, Office Workers
Context — Context - 3 story base relates to district development and pedestrian scale. Promenade relates to river scale and fluidity	3	Activated Pathway	Office amenities activate a garden streetscape and hide the multistory garage from pedestrian view.	Cafeteria, fitness center, conferencing, training , along side landscaping, outdoor dining, water features, seating and lawn area.	Office Workers, General Public
	4	Recreational	Garage rooftop serves as the platform for a variety of recreational uses, for both the office workers and by reservation the general public.	Soccer, softball, tennis, picnicking, along with restrooms.	Office Workers, General Public (with reservations)
	5	Park	A large circular park contains an outdoor amphitheater	Outdoor amphitheater, landscaping, water features, seating and lawn area.	Office Workers, General Public
	6	Entry Plaza	Entry plaza invites you into The Canyon, an activated pathway, that connects thru the entire project	Major auto and pedestrian entry point.	General Public, Office Workers

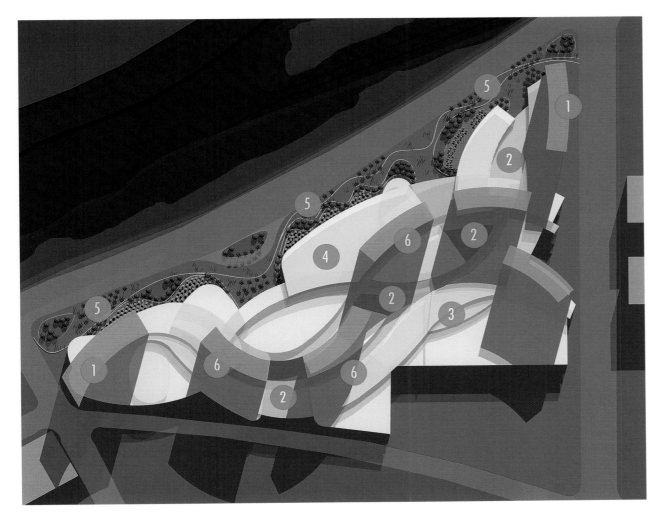

Imagine....sitting on an elevated terraces, sipping coffee, watching the flow of people walking by with a gentle river as a backdrop.

The dynamic flow of the adjacent river was the inspiration for this large retail entertainment complex. The place diagram is a series of parallel "streets" which guide the flow of people through the project. On the interior, these "streets" consist of a sequence of plazas and pathways that flow from one end of the project to the other. This affords a pacing and curving elegance which maintain an interest and excitement as one explores the complex.

The exterior is where the "street" takes on a real grandeur. A grand promenade follows the river's edge, it is a fluid combination of landscape, enriched broad walkways, dinning terraces, retail shops, and event spaces. It is designed as a destination in itself.

Meandering Edge - Metroplex

			Place Type	Description	Activators	Target Users
Formal Rational	Project forms reflect the fluid dynamics of the adjacent river, as well as the interwoven nature of a neighborhood development.	**1**	Iconic Form	Iconic Hotel towers anchor project forms	Distant views of iconic forms create signature landmarks.	Long and Medium distance views by pedestrians, car passengers
Context	Context - 3-story base relates to district development and pedestrian scale. Promenade relates to river scale and fluidity.	**2**	Atriums	Interior atrium spaces become public plazas, each with a unique focus, some on a concentrated retail theme, others on interactive art features.	Retail, seating-gathering areas, theme based activities, interactive artwork, landscape.	Shoppers, general public, hotel guests, condo residents
		3	Entertainment Anchor	The rooftop becomes a sculptural entertainment area.	Gaming Arcade, Cinemas, Pop Culture Exhibits and Events.	Shoppers, general public, hotel guests, condo residents
		4	Activity Anchor	The rooftop becomes a sculptural indoor and outdoor dining area.	Restaurants with river and distant city views. Food court with interior mall atrium view	Shoppers, general public, hotel guests, condo residents
		5	Activated Pathway - Promenade	A series of serpentine forms echo the meandering flow of the adjacent river. With in these forms restaurants, cafes, shops, and major mall entry portals create a promenade along the rivers edge.	Restaurants, cafes, shops, view of river and pedestrians	Shoppers, general public, hotel guests, condo residents
		6	Activated Pathway- Interior	Retail lines both sides of this interior street.	Retail, seating-gathering areas, food kiosks, shopping kiosks, artwork.	Shoppers, general public, hotel guests, condo residents

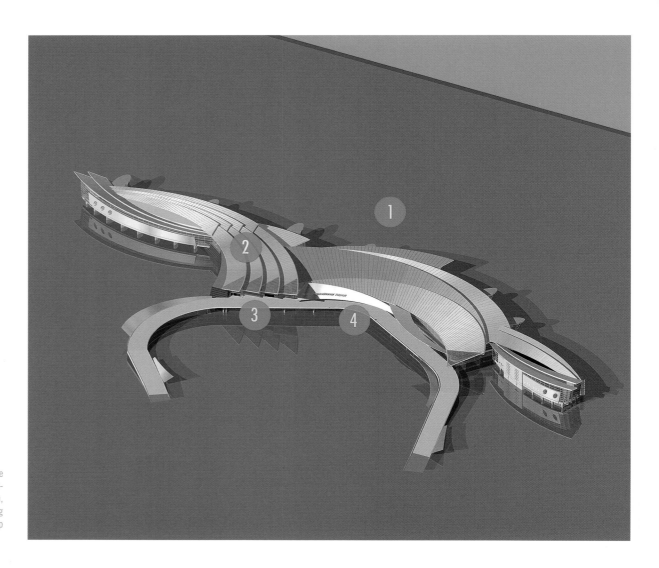

All airports are modern versions of the "city gates". The intention here was to create a gate which became a symbolic reflection of Jeju Island's cultural heritage. As an icon, it needed to be experienced from the air, from the arriving passenger's point of view, as well as at the drop off/pick up area from a car, taxi, or mass transit.

Portal to the Winds - Jeju Int. Airport		Place Type	Description	Activators	Target Users
	1	Iconic- Metaphoric Form	The wind forms are symbolic of the fierce winds of Jeju Island, and the dynamics of flight	Broad symbol for Jeju Islands, both from the air and the ground	Airline passengers, general public
Major Formal Rational — The wind forms are symbolic of the fierce winds of Jeju Island, and the dynamics of flight	2	Atrium - Activated Pathway	Dramatically curving walls and ceilings continue the wind theme throughout the travelers experience	Waiting areas, retail, cafes, restaurants.	Airline passengers
Context — Context - Strong and unique form surrounded by paving. Remote from adjacent development	3	Entry Icon	The roof forms aggressively cantilever creating an iconic signature for the international departures entrance and drop off.	Drop off, major entrance to facility	Airline passengers, general public
	4	Activated Pathway	Broad curving roofs provide shelter for departing passengers	Drop off, secondary entrances to facility	Airline passengers, general public

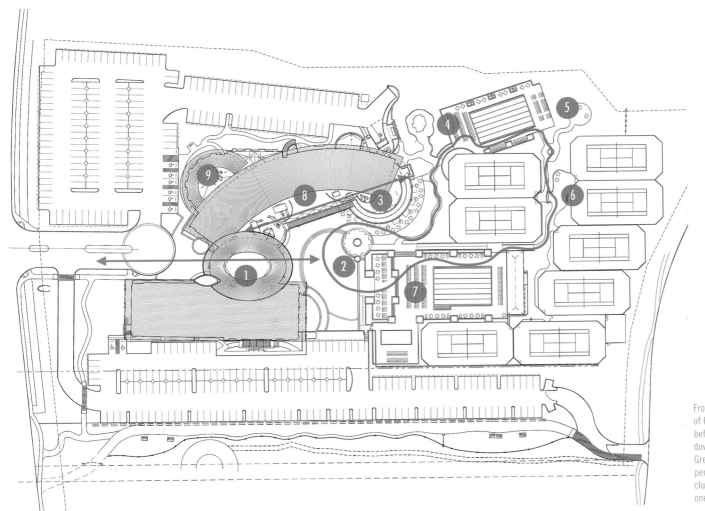

From the moment you walk into the 3-story lobby of PAC San Diego a generous landscape unfolds before your eyes. This indoor space cascades down a grand arcing stair, and out unto the Great Lawn. This indoor-outdoor relationship permeates the entire experience of using the club and creates a constant sense of place as one navigates its corridors and major spaces.

Sinew - Carmel Valley Club

		Place Type	Description	Activators	Target Users
Formal Rational	Muscular curving forms are metaphors of the physical nature of an athletic club	1 Atrium	Central atrium is the symbolic heart of the complex, and is the main entry point for the project.	Circulation hub, viewpoint to great lawn, pool landscape and mountains beyond	Club members
		2 Great Lawn	7,000 sf oval sunken lawn area. The great lawn serves both as the "heart" of the project landscape, and as a highly functional outdoor event area. It is adjacent to the Heritage Tree sitting area.	Outdoor parties, games, kid's events, barbeques, fitness classes.	Club members adults, families, kids, non-member events
Context	Context- Stucco material and color, along with sloping roofs relates to neighborhood.	3 Activity Anchor	Indoor outdoor café sits at the crossroads of all major exterior circulation and the Family Pool area	Café, outdoor dining deck	Club members adults, families, kids
		4 Quiet Place	Adult pool is a quiet oasis for swimming laps or reading and sunbathing	Adult pool, seating in sun and shade.	Adult club members
		5 Mystery Place	Quiet hidden picnic area. This area is surrounded by lush landscaping, and is up hill from the adjacent pathway	BBQ, tables, and seating	Small groups of members seeking relaxation
		6 Quiet Place	Landscapes social space next to tennis courts.	Umbrella tables, and seating	Small groups of members seeking relaxation
		7 Activity Place	Family pool area has a multitude of swim activities, as well as sunbathing.	Adult pool, seating in sun and shade, restrooms, pool toys, adjacent to café	Club members adults, families, kids
		8 Activated Pathway	Interior and exterior pathways link to each other and form a loop, creating an episodic adventure.	Lobby, locker rooms, program spaces, café.	Club members
		9 Activity Anchor	Day spa creates a public activity anchor.	Day spa brings the general public inside the facility	Club members, general public

Amidst the drama of two massive waves crashing overhead, the true heart of this project lies in the glass volume of the lobby. It is the moment of calm before both the music and the waves begin their inevitable dance that creates the tension and, oddly, a sense of protection from the chaos of the world outside.

		Place Type	Description	Activators	Target Users
Crashing Waves - Tongyeong Concert Hall	1	Atrium	Atrium created by the void under the powerful crashing wave forms	Lobby spaces, café, bar	Concert goers, students, general public
Formal Rational — Two massive crashing wave forms relate to Isang Yun's music, the project's Oceanside location, and the relationship of the two Koreas	2	Aspirational Icon	Arcing glass forms are metaphors of the energy created by two waves crashing together. The glass forms extend above the waves to add vertical drama.		Long and medium distance views by general public and tourists.
Context — Context - Strong and unique form rises from a tree covered hill. Remote from adjacent development	3	Iconic- Metaphoric Form	Two massive crashing wave forms relate to Isang Yun's music, the project's Oceanside location, and the relationship of the two Koreas		Long and medium distance views by general public and tourists.
	4	Cultural Anchor	600 seat outdoor performance space carved into the side of the cliffs.	Outdoor performances, adjacent to outdoor café space, distant views	General public, concert goers
	5	Cultural Icon	Arcing glass forms create a memorial to Isang Yun	Memorial exhibition	General public, concert goers
	6	View Point	Viewpoint to ocean and distant mountainous islands, also serves as outdoor event space.	Distant views	General public, concert goers